THE TUMOUR IN THE WHALE

A Universal Original

A friend of a friend who is a Readymix driver suspected his wife of infidelity. One day, he made sure that she thought he was going to be miles away, and then drove past his house. Sure enough, the bedroom curtains were drawn, and outside stood a brand-new Triumph convertible. Sickened at this display of opulence, our driver had a brilliant idea on the spur of the moment – he drove round the block and prepared his load of cement. Then he returned, positioned his lorry, extended the chute, reversed the barrel and filled the Triumph convertible with Readymix. As he packed up to drive away, a foxy little man came out of his house, climbed on to a bicycle, and pedalled briskly away in the opposite direction.

The Tumour in the Whale

A Collection of Modern Myths

By
Rodney Dale

Foreword
George Melly

Illustrations
Bill Tidy

UNIVERSAL

A UNIVERSAL BOOK
published by
the Paperback Division of W. H. ALLEN & Co. Ltd.

A Universal Book
Published in 1978
by the Paperback Division of
W. H. Allen & Co. Ltd
A Howard and Wyndham Company
44 Hill Street, London W1X 8LB

Copyright © 1978 by Rodney Dale
Foreword copyright © 1978 by George Melly

Printed in Great Britain by
Cox & Wyman Ltd, London, Reading and Fakenham

ISBN 0 426 18710 5

To my Mother, with love
and in loving memory
of my Father

Contents

Acknowledgements

Thank you, George, for identifying the Whale Tumour Story and for your foreword; thank you, Bill, for your illustrations; thank you both for your interest in the project.

Thank you, Joan Gray, for the many helpful suggestions you have made since the book was a twinkle in the eye of *Interface*, and thank you, Cambridge Consultants, for *Interface*.

Thank you, Joyce Wrightson, for typing the text and helping it along its way.

Thank you Judith, and Timothy, Henry and Malcolm, for your support, encouragement and understanding.

Many people in the last twenty-five years have said things which I have stored, 'photographically lined on the tablets of my mind'. Apart from those above, and other members of my family, inspiration has been derived from: Marjorie Allen, Roger Barrington-Styles, John Bathurst, Roger Bennison, Peter Bill, Allen Boothroyd, Mike Boursnell, Althea Braithwaite, Roger Briggs, David Brooke, Fred Brown, John Chilton, Ray Clark, Dudley Clews, Chris Cook, George Cooper, Hugo Davenport, Anne Davies, Len Douglas, Richard Duke, Bushy Eiloart, Tim Eiloart, Mike Everitt, Colin Fisher, John Forster, John Galpin, Val Galpin, Janet Hales, Elna Hoare, Mike Hoare, Adrian Horne, Andrew Houston, Don Ingleton, Gerry Johnson, Chris Lakin, Hugh Lindeman, Maurice Lynn, Tommy Maddox, Michael Mansfield, Stanley Mansfield, Peter Manuel, Alan McCombie, Jim Miller, Stuart Miller, Don Moss, Roger Mottram, Laurence O'Toole, Keith Padbury, Mervyn Parry, Robert Phillips, Roy Pitches, Deric Platt, Mark Platt, Carole Pook, Alex Popple, Steve Puttick, Charles Rogers, Roger Rowland, George Sassoon, Susie Sassoon, Sue Schimmels, Frank Sheridan, Tony Short, Clive Sinclair, Shenton Smith, Bob Snodgrass, Chris South, David Southward, Gerry Staite, John Stanford, Stanley Storr, Strangers at parties, in pubs and on trains, Steve Temple,

Ted Tetley, Rodney Tibbs, Michael Till, Rosemary Vicary, Hugo de Waal, Sue Whitby, Ray Woodman and Harry Wrightson.

I am also grateful to the following for permission to quote from their works: Russel Ash *Fact or Fiction?* *Reader's Digest*; Briggs and Tongue *Folktales of England* Routledge & Kegan Paul; *The Secret Life of Salvador Dali* Vision Press; Bergen Evans *The Natural History of Nonsense* and *The Spoor of Spooks* Michael Joseph; Grundy *Punch* reproduced by permission of *Punch*; Hogg and Weeks *Military Small-arms of the Twentieth Century* (3rd edition) Arms and Armour Press; Lord Montagu of Beaulieu *The Gilt and the Gingerbread* Michael Joseph and Sphere Books; Eric Partridge *The Shaggy Dog Story*; Enid Porter *Cambridgeshire Customs and Folklore* Routledge & Kegan Paul; H. Allen Smith *The Compleat Practical Joker* Arthur Barker; James Sutherland *The Oxford Book of Literary Anecdotes* Oxford University Press; Symons *Buller's Campaign* Cresset Press; E. S. Turner *The Phoney War* Michael Joseph.

Foreword

Materializing as I do in the very first paragraph of this book, I can hardly pretend to surprise at its existence. There is, however, a deal of difference between an *idea* for a book and its realization, and here I can express nothing but admiration. That same fine July evening of which the author speaks may have contained the moment of its conception but, if Rodney Dale will allow me to change his sex (metaphorically), there is a world of difference between the few moments necessary to father a child and the months of gestation and effort needed to bring it into the world.

The 'whale-meat story', or whale tumour syndrome, is part of the collective mythology of the band-waggon, a vehicle in which the John Chilton Feetwarmers and myself spend so much of our middle-age. I think it was John himself who first, in reaction to some contemporary but equally unlikely tale, resurrected that moment of horror on the wartime dresser which is to become explicit in the opening pages of this book, but the rest of us had either heard and forgotten it, or were able to produce similar instances of the need to believe the impossible and to attempt to insist on its veracity by citing its source. At all events it did little more than provide us with a convenient yard-stick, and the source of a handy phrase to indicate scepticism. Nor would it have gone further if I had not happened to explain its meaning to Rodney Dale in that Cambridge inn-yard one fine summer evening.

Rodney has seen fit to describe me in flattering terms – to evoke both Dr Johnson *and* Max Miller in a single paragraph is little short of fulsome. He chooses, however, to appear only as a witness, albeit a potentially constructive one. Here then are a few observations:

Rodney is one of those rare, enviable creatures who bridge, with no apparent strain, those Two Cultures as defined by C. P. Snow. On the one hand he has a knowledge of computers, science, mathematics and logic, and on the other a sense of fantasy and absurdity verging on the manic.

Forced to choose a spiritual ancestor for him, I would propose Lewis Carroll. Dale's own grasp of logic indeed frequently leads him into a Wave of Carrollian absurdity. He has a habit of pursuing an ill-considered statement with the obsessive air of the Bellman on the track of the Snark. It is this quality which convinces me that this book and its author were destined for each other, and to think of myself as a mere catalyst.

Method and obsession are the horses that pull Rodney's mental carriage. Dressed, for jazz functions at any rate, with neat Bohemian panache and a somewhat excessive fondness for shades of mauve, sporting a well-behaved beard, he could be taken at first glance for a 'modern' painter in a *Punch* cartoon of the middle 'twenties. This façade is however betrayed by his eyes which, while hiding behind his glasses, comb reality like radar beams, registering instantly the passing of whales with or without tumours. Here in front of you are his findings, methodical and dotty, and written down with a crisp asperity which those of us who know him will recognize as exactly his tone of voice.

There is no need for me here to pontificate on the need for absurd mythology in modern man – Rodney Dale has himself performed that task admirably, and happily in Bill Tidy (himself a formidable creator of tripe-manufacturers and clog-dancers as insanely obsessional in their beliefs as his subjects here) he has found the ideal illustrator.

Ahead of you is a museum of credulity. You will, of course, recognize its absurdity – except in the case of just one or two stories which you happen to know, irrefutably, and on excellent authority (a friend of the wife's brother? a cousin of the man who mends the washing machine?) are absolutely true ...

George Melly

Prologue

It was a perfect July evening; George Melly was to perform at the Guildhall, Cambridge, and we had met beforehand in the yard of the Eagle Tavern in Bene't Street.

George sat on a plastic beer-crate, wearing his Max Miller suit, with hat, cigar, cane and grin – exuding the charisma of a twentieth-century Samuel Johnson. Discussing some anecdote, he said: 'That's a whale-tumour story ... Do you know what a whale-tumour story is?' At that time, I didn't. He continued:

> During the war, when whale-meat was offered as a substitute for beef, a woman bought some whale-meat steak, took it home, and put it on a plate before preparing it for the oven. Her husband was sitting in the living-room, and suddenly a movement in the kitchen caught his eye ... on investigation, they found that it was the whale-meat, which contained a live tumour, gently throbbing ...

> A whale-tumour story is one of those that people swear is true – it happened to a friend of theirs, but you never actually meet this friend. And you keep hearing of the same thing happening to friends up and down the country ...

After that, I started to notice and collect whale-tumour stories (WTSs), and the first fruits of the labour, with some thoughts arising, are presented here.

The stories I tell are of three types, as follows:

(a) 'I saw ...' or 'I did ...' means exactly that – I am speaking from personal experience.

(b) 'A friend (or some named person) saw ...' means that to the best of my knowledge and belief what they said was true.

(c) 'A friend of a friend (foaf) saw ...' means that it has been reported from several quarters, that its provenance is shady, that it is almost certainly a WTS.

You may ask why I include true stories. The answer,

simply, is in the interest of truth. If I say here that something has happened to me, then that is true. If you have heard that the same thing has happened to others, then either that's a coincidence, the likelihood of which you may judge from the story itself, or my experience has turned into a WTS.

Or, of course, you may find me reporting as type c an incident which happened to you – in that case, you're the original, elusive foaf.

The recording of the form of a story at a particular time should be another useful achievement. We can see stories being modified, updated, planished and embroidered to suit the times – the 'elephant and the motor car' (Chapter 8) is an example of this. By recording a story in mid-1977, we have a fixed point to which its past and future may be referred.

It has been suggested that this book will put a stop to the WTS, since those who read it will give up telling them, and those who have read it will laugh at the persistent tellers. I don't think that is likely. Persistent tellers will continue to assert that they know the person to whom it happened, and I suppose that I will have to bear the attacks of those who are deeply offended that I should dare to question what they *know* to be true stories – having heard them so many times, presumably. Alternatively, finding that his favourite story is here, the raconteur may aver proudly that this book is the very authority upon which his story is based – that he was the original foaf. But in his heart of hearts he will know that, as before, he is unlikely to be challenged, even though his audience, having read this book, may not be quite as acceptant as in the past.

There is a certain autobiographical leaning in my text, and many of the tales relate to the Cambridge in which I have lived for nearly forty years, and to its University. I'm not apologizing – just warning you, and telling you that I realize it.

As far as I know, this is the first time that an attempt has been made at amassing WTSs; their classification is therefore not immutable; the 'elephant and the motor car' for example could be either in Chapter 7 or in Chapter 8 – I happened to choose the latter.

However, some pattern has started to emerge, and if readers are kind enough to send me their omitted variants –

or, indeed, stories I have missed – I will do my best to carry the work forward; see Tailpiece p. 169.

Rodney Dale
Bar Hill, Cambridge

August 1977

NOTE

Since I completed this script, Philip Ward has published *A Dictionary of Common Fallacies*; I commend it to you (97).

Mr Ward points out that I may use the word 'myth' wrongly. Sorry about that, purists; it's alluringly alliterative and I'm not averse from the Humpty Dumpty syndrome.

Introductory Survey

> It is necessary always to aim at being interesting rather
> than at being exact; for the spectator forgives everything
> except dreariness
>
> Voltaire

The existence of the WTS – though not under that banner –
has been recognized, but its characteristics have not been
properly explored until now. For example, Richard M.
Dorson writes (11):

> The joke, the shaggy dog, the tall tale, the numskull
> story abound among educated city folk and deserve ac-
> ceptance in the corpus of folktales. Little attempt has yet
> been made to gather and examine these forms although
> Eric Partridge did devote a book to the Shaggy Dog Story
> ... [66]. The humorous, modern story lore belongs not to
> regions but to mobile society and easily crosses the At-
> lantic between England and America. Macabre legends
> also thrive in the modern metropolis. The newly un-
> covered modern legend of 'The Stolen Corpse' [Chapter
> 1] was first reported in England in 1963, and within the
> year it had been recorded in the U.S.

That is obviously a start, though the WTS is by no means
confined to 'educated city folk' – Dorson seems to have some
stereotype in mind – and there is confusion between the
'humorous story' and the 'macabre legend'.

Collectors such as Briggs (10 & 11), Emrich (28) and Stith
Thompson (87) have recognized what we would call WTSs,
but have no common name for them. In their detailed
analyses of legend, the WTS, the myth of today, seems to
have fallen by the wayside. Having said that, it would be fair
to ask how one recognizes a WTS anyway. One way is to

become familiar with the genre, by reading this book, for example. But first, let us have a look at some classes of story, which will help us to put the WTS into context.

The joke

is presented with the idea of making the hearer laugh. Sometimes, the presenter is clearly out to make his audience laugh – he may be billed as 'the world's funniest man' (what a title to live up to), he may be introduced as a comedian, he may draw a cartoon or comic strip. All these are signals which warn the audience: 'my intention is to make you laugh'. Sometimes the material is presented deadpan, and the presenter does not mind (ostensibly at least) whether or not his audience laughs. The larger the audience, the more likely is someone to catch on sooner rather than later; if the audience is one person, the deadpan joke is a leg-pull.

Jokes come in all shapes and sizes. Consider Groucho Marx's elegant:

What? Spring in the air and fall in the lake?

or the multi-pun line:

Sir Matt Busby has been redecorated and will henceforth be known as Lord Glossy Boater.

or the entomological:

When the prof asked the zoologist where he had been the previous day, he replied that he had been out in the field, studying *Phyllostomus grylloides*.

At the sorting-office, they open all the mail addressed to Father Christmas, and one year found one from an old-age pensioner (sorry, senior citizen) living alone, who asked for five pounds so that he could give himself a Christmas treat. The supervisor was very touched by this letter, and pinned it up on the canteen notice-board, with a box beneath it for contributions. When he counted the money, it came to £3.72, so he changed it into four pound notes by donating the difference, and sent it off to the old man, 'with the compliments of Santa Claus'. The next day, there was a note from the old man: 'Dear Santa, thank you very much for the money – but I reckon those thieving gits at the Post Office must have nicked one of the notes.'

There's the humour of pathos, laughter equals tears, the clown wants to play Hamlet. (If he ever does, we're not told who wins.)

Each nation has an associated one about whom it tells jokes. Jugoslavs tell Lala jokes, Germans tell Scottish jokes (as a surrogate for telling Jewish jokes?) the Danes tell Aahrus jokes, Canadians tell Newfie jokes and the English tell Irish jokes.

Many of these are one-liners, and concern such topics as the Irishman who bought a black and white dog because he thought that the licence would be cheaper.

Be that as it may, the Irish do have an endearing logic of their own, and I will illustrate this with a true story.

There is an Irish builder called Frank on whose expertise I call from time to time. I was having some trouble with leaking gutters, so I asked Frank if he could come along with his longest ladder, for I live in a three-storey house. He arrived, and I asked him how long his ladder was.

'Twenty-five feet, if it's fully extended, but unfortunately you can't fully extend it.'

'Oh, why's that?'

'It's broken.'

However, he was able to get on to the roof, and found two problems – the gutters were full of tennis balls (easily remedied), and the lead was split (not so easy).

'It's a plumber's job – I'll have to get George in, he's a plumber. You know George, he delivers your milk.'

'Oh, yes.'

However, the removal of the tennis balls made a great improvement, and it was only when I thought that a little preventive maintenance wouldn't come amiss that I called Frank again.

'Oh, yes. I need George. Tell you what, I'll see if he can come out with me on Saturday morning.'

Apparently he could, for we were awoken by a scraping of ladders on walls on Saturday morning. I kept out of the way, not wishing to hold up the proceedings. However, at the appropriate hour I went out to offer coffee and biscuits, and was surprised to find George the plumber holding the ladder, and Frank on the roof doing the job. When they'd finished, I asked Frank why he'd needed a plumber to hold the ladder if he was going to do the job himself.

The explanation seemed perfectly logical:

'Well, you see, George can't stand heights.'

Irish stories are not a new phenomenon. There was a story current at the turn of the century (34) wherein some Irish builders had been instructed to build a wall round a ruined church to protect it. To save materials, they drew on the fabric of the ruined church.

The practical joke

is a perfectly-defined genre which some, nevertheless, seek to ignore, though they will readily admit to the existence of 'pranks' which, when examined, turn out to be practical jokes. H. Allen Smith's monograph on the subject (82) was published a quarter of a century ago; it is, however, an important authority and sourcebook for many stories which have turned up in other guises since it was written – some as WTSs.

In 1965, John Forster advertised himself in the *Mensa Bulletin* as he was seeking a job as an accountant: Cambridge Consultants, needing one and naturally drawn towards anyone advertising himself in *MB*, took him on. John started on 8th March, and on 1st April we received a letter from the Floral Research Association seeking our advice on preserving cut flowers, to fight 'the ever-increasing competition from the "plastic" flower market.' We replied to the FRA that we would be delighted to be engaged on this fascinating problem, but heard no more. John hadn't wasted much time; we found later that the 'FRA' happened to be at his parents' address.

Later that year, Althea Braithwaite, who had just started to manage my printing company, received a charming letter purporting to come from the Vicar of Swaffham Prior and thanking her in advance for her generous donation to his repair fund. This worried Althea, but we worked out that the letter must have been sent by John, who had found a record of her visit to the church in the visitors' book.

Now, the reason that he had visited Swaffham Prior was that he collects postmarks. It was therefore natural that he should have noticed that some of his letters (for some irrelevant reason which never came to light) were travelling all round Will's mother's before they were delivered to him. This story got into the papers. And that was our chance.

We printed a one-off letterhead for the 'Union of Post Office Operatives' and wrote John a letter from the 'Convening Shop Steward' saying that if he didn't retract his vile imputations of Post Office inefficiency, the whole of the Post Office would come out on strike. John arrived at work the following day looking distinctly ill.

Our preparations had been thorough; the type had been set for the letterhead, and distributed immediately afterwards. The materials used for make-ready had been taken home and burnt. But we had made one mistake. The piece of paper on which we had printed the letterhead was a sample sheet, and had a note of its provenance printed on the bottom – this we had cut off and put in the dustbin. John went through several inky dustbins that evening, looking for evidence – and found this narrow, matching strip of paper. He deserved to.

A practical joke can become a WTS quite easily. The following may be correctly ascribed, but when one hears it told of, for example, a member of the French resistance in a train with two large German ladies, one becomes suspicious.

> The present [1953] Lord Halifax, formerly Ambassador to the United States, was travelling to Bath in a railway compartment, also occupied by two very prim middle-aged ladies who were strangers to each other. The train entered a tunnel and the compartment was engulfed in darkness. Lord Halifax placed the back of his hand to his mouth and kissed it noisily several times. When the train reached the station he arose, doffed his hat, and said, 'To which of you charming ladies am I indebted for the delightful incident in the tunnel?' He left them glaring hatefully at each other. (82)

The shaggy dog story
is a species of deadpan joke which rambles on and on, and may reach its punchline before the fact that it is meant to be funny is detected. By some coincidence, it is twenty-five years for the shaggy dog story, as it is for the practical joke,

since a monograph on the subject appeared (66), compiled by the indefatigable Eric Partridge. It is a valuable work of identification, but our familiarity with the genre has mellowed since 1953, and we are better able to see a shaggy dog coming when it does.

At a 'local' in one of London's suburbs – so far as that goes, it might equally well have been in Paris or a New York suburb – a regular, of twenty years' moderate drinking, entered a new phase of enjoyment when a stranger began to frequent the bar. Not that he was interested in the stranger but in the dog that always accompanied him and did so much to enliven the evening.

The first time the stranger and his dog came into the room, which, in an older tradition fast dying out, possessed rather a good piano, the man ordered a pint o' bitter, sat down on a stool, patted the dog's head, and quietly urged him to 'play something for us, Smoky. Something lively. This dump's like a morgue, we must do something about it.'

To the amazement of the regulars and the preparing-to-be-resentful barman, the dog sedately walked to the piano and adjusted the stool. Without looking round for preliminary applause, nor in fact receiving any, it started to play a very catchy thing from the most popular musical comedy of the moment. The animal played very well, without any irritating mannerisms or large, pretentious gestures. On being asked to 'play us another, do!' and seeing that this was not mere politeness but genuine appreciation, the modest executant played two other numbers from the same 'musical'.

For many evenings this sort of thing continued. The regulars would ask, now for 'Nelly Dean' or some other sentimental ballad, now for a specifically Cockney song, such as 'My Old Dutch', and occasionally for a more classical piece. One night, whilst everyone was listening raptly to a most artistic rendering of Handel's 'Largo', a famous music-hall manager strolled in to quench a raging thirst. Suddenly the visitor realized that, whoever was playing, he certainly 'knew his stuff'. He was amazed to see that it was a dog, a very ordinary looking dog. 'Surely not,' he muttered to himself, 'it's far too early for that.'

'Plays well, don't you think?' remarked the dog's owner.

'He sure does. Would he play "The Warsaw Concerto"?'

'Piece of cake. Hey there, play "The Warsaw" for the gentlemen, will you? And don't pull your punches.'

The dog played this spectacular piece with spectacular virtuosity.

'Anything else you'd like?'

'Yes, Liszt's "Hungarian Rhapsody" – that very fast, difficult one all the most florid pianists love to play – and so seldom can.' (That'll fox him, he thought; this bloke won't know the meaning of 'florid' ... not at all sure I do myself; anyway, the dog'll never have heard of Liszt, but if I'm wrong, it'll prove that the creature's good, so good that I'll sign him up.)

The 'canine pianist' – already the astute music-hall manager was composing an advertisement – had no trouble in dealing with this example of musical pyrotechnics. Bewildered, the manager, not because he wished to know but simply because he hated to give himself away to these simpletons of the suburbs, blurted:

'Yes, the dog is good; in fact, marvellous.'

Pause –

'By the way, can the animal orchestrate?'

'Orchestrate? Don't be silly! Haven't you noticed that my dog is a bitch?'

And Partridge adds a footnote:

That, more or less, is how the story is usually told; that, exactly, is the wording of the owner's final speech. By the majority, the story is thought to stand very satisfactorily on its external merits. It does. By the Greek scholar and by the etymologist, however, the conclusion is enjoyed for another reason.

Quite.

The ghost story
may be told for various reasons – to exemplify the existence of the supernatural, to challenge the hearer's credulity, to make the flesh creep, or just to entertain. Just as the billing 'the world's funniest man' is not calculated to help the billee,

so does the ghost story find it increasingly difficult to live up to any promise of 'spine-chilling eeriness', etc. The ghost story shares with the whale tumour story the characteristic that, if there is any laughter in it, it is secondary to the theme: the laughter in no way detracts from the 'truth' of the story, or turns it into a joke.

Many of the colleges of Cambridge are allegedly haunted; the following tale belongs to Jesus College (38):

There was a man called Byfield, a Roundhead parson billeted in Jesus during the Civil War. Cromwell's soldiers had little respect for learning and most of the scholars had fled the college rather than brave their jeers and taunts. One of the few to remain, a Fellow named Allen, had the room above Byfield's and night after night the ignorant and superstitious Roundhead heard him chanting his strange formulae, convinced he was communing with his Master, the Devil. After a while, Byfield realized he no longer heard Allen's heavy human footsteps leaving the room at night and stumbling down the stair in the dark, but only a quick, light pattering. One night, unable to stand the suspense any longer, Byfield tentatively opened the door to see a huge black cat trot past. Trembling with his own daring, he crept up the stairs to Allen's room which was empty ... save for a few papers covered with mysterious and evil signs.

Night after night Byfield lay in bed listening to the in-human footsteps pattering past his door at midnight and returning stealthily at dawn. One by one, soldiers billeted in the college died. One night, Byfield could stand no more. He crept out of his door and took a large horse-pistol from the rack outside the nearby armoury. He waited for the cat and, when he saw it, fired full in its chest. With an unearthly scream the animal disappeared into the night, and Byfield returned to his room convinced that God's will had been done. Next morning Allen's body was discovered in a grove of trees by Kings Ditch, where the troopers went to draw water for their horses. A great horse-pistol bullet had torn a hole through his chest and a trail of blood, thick gouts of it, led from the armoury by the foot of the stair to the grove where the body lay. Suicide. That was the verdict. The necromancer, unable

24

to bear the weight of his own evil, had shot himself in his room and dragged himself outside to die under the stars with which he had kept his unholy communion. That night, the body was laid out in Allen's customary room, above Byfield's bed. Byfield was gripped with horror as he lay in the paralysing silence. Desperately, he prayed for forgiveness and, as he finished, heard the door of the room above open and soft, pattering footsteps descend the stairs. He steeled himself to go to Allen's room: empty. No dead man with shot-mangled chest and staring eyes lay on the bed. Then he heard it: soft, furry footsteps, stalking him. He swung round to see the cat, eyes ablaze, poised to spring. 'Oh my God, make haste for my help,' gabbled Byfield, sinking down beside the empty bed. His hands closed on the stiff corpse of Thomas Allen, where he was discovered the next morning, raving. He died within the year.

Many ghost stories are incredibly wenge – that is to say, both the teller and the listener begin to glaze and lose interest before the end; or the end, when it arrives, makes them wish that they hadn't started.

As an example of a wenge ghost story, I would quote that of a London theatre, which 'was reputed to harbour the ghost of an irritable ex-Thespian in astrakhan collar that used to be seen in the vicinity of the manager's office.' The manager said that he had no doubt that the place was haunted, though he had never seen the ghost himself, but had talked to other people who had. Yes.

Folk tales
very often turn out to be wenge as well. Consider:

The Good Magpie

There was once a gentleman who used to ride on horse-back every day. One day he had occasion to call at a house by the roadside, where a woman and her little boy lived. Whilst he was talking to the woman, he saw that she was making the oven hot, and the little boy said to him, 'Mother's holing the oven to put me in.'

But the gentleman thought the boy was only joking, so he took no heed and rode away. But he had not gone far before a magpie crossed his path, and kept flying in front of his horse, and would not go away. So at last he thought that the magpie wanted him to turn back. So he rode straight back to the house, and when he got there he found that the woman had gone and that the poor little boy was roasting in the oven.

The Man Who Got Into His Cart

One May I met and stopped to talk to an elderly carter in a Quantock lane. After mutual admiration of the hill pony I rode, and his solid Shire mare, we went on to discuss their ways. Yes, they had both been difficult that day, and so, all unasked for, out came this tale: "'Tis May, you see,' said the carter. '*Always troublesome they are then.* I don't never trust'n, not even the old 'oss yur. I've worked she twenty years tew. My wife she have an old uncle over to they Blackdowns and they were carting stones to *mend their Church.* Uphill 'tis and a nasty piece of road – they was those days, all stones – and there was a a bit of a bank down over. I'd awalk any 'oss up there and down over but there was a carter, he did get intew the cart see – and *summat* gave his 'osses a fright and he was killed outright. In May 'twas. There's a verse over at the church there. No; I don't like May. Never tell what a 'oss will take and do.' (11)

I'm not knocking the collectors and classifiers of folk tales, by the way; I'm just pointing out that, out of context, folk tales are not very tellable.

The old wives' tale

or folk belief may be in one of two sharply-defined categories: either it contains some truth or it doesn't. With the current trend towards mysticism and debunking of science, many old wives' tales are being got out and polished in an attempt to show that our ancestors 'knew a thing or two', or 'weren't stupid'. Of the sort which we may surely discount is the belief that worms cause toothache:

If a worm eat the tooth, take acorn meal and henbane seed and wax, of all equally much, mingle these together, work into a wax candle and burn it, let it reek into the mouth, put a black cloth under, then will the worms fall out (22).

Or again:

An approved remedy for a wolfe in a womans brest. Take crabbs when they be thorough ripe roste ym and when ya be thorough rosted spread ym on a cloth and lukewarme lay ym unto the sore brest and it will help the woman greined it must be drest twice a day and when you pull of the plaster snatch it of hastily and perhaps ye shall see ye worm come forth or appear yn if you can take hold of it pull it out if you may be suffered (92).

On the other hand, there are those tales with more substance, such as that chewing willow trees (*Salix* sp) cures headaches – for has not the tree given its name to the salicylic acid which it contains, and is this not the principle of aspirin?

Popular fallacies

are an extension of old wives' tales, and begin to take us away from our subject of interest, for many popular fallacies are beliefs which are never articulated. If, however, they are brought into conversation, they nearly always have some foaf to support them – someone whose hair turned white overnight, or who has seen the Indian rope trick. People do not like their pet beliefs being challenged.

Essential for students of popular fallacies are Ackerman (1) and Evans (30 & 31), though the former, some half a century old, contains many popular fallacies which one hardly recognizes as such today:

That a Ventriloquist Talks in his Stomach

The etymology of this word has a great deal to answer for, as it no doubt keeps the popular idea alive. Certain animals, to wit the lobster and the crayfish, have teeth in their stomachs; but, as far as we know, they do not possess the power of producing audible sound by means of those organs.

On this subject, Prof. Huxley, FRS, says: 'What is called *ventriloquism* (speaking from the belly), and is not uncommonly ascribed to a mysterious power of producing voice somewhere else than in the larynx, depends entirely upon the accuracy with which the performer can simulate sounds of a particular character, and upon the skill with which he can suggest a belief in the existence of the causes of these sounds . . .

WE CAN SEE YOUR BELLY BUTTON MOVING!

The Rev Dr Brewer also provides good value in explaining the world around us (9):

Q. *Why is not* old beer *and* strong porter *made* sour *by lightning?*

A. Because the *fermentation is more complete*; and, therefore, is less affected by electrical influence.

Q. *Show the wisdom of God in making* air *a* bad conductor.

A. If air were a *good conductor* (like iron and stone) heat would be drawn *so rapidly* from our body, that we should be *chilled to death*.

Really popular fallacies, such as the superiority of brown eggs over white eggs, may never die. Often, they are harmless enough, save that, as Goethe said, 'Nothing is more harmful to a new truth than an old error.'

Popular fallacies may easily become WTSs. Enid Porter writes (69):

> Generations of men have been informed that MAs and Doctors may play marbles on the steps of the Senate House [Cambridge] on Degree Days, and that anyone wearing Lincoln Green has the indisputable right to practise archery in Petty Cury. So long in fact have these two fictions been maintained that they are now almost believed as based on historical fact.

I remember hearing that, according to a statute dating from the time of Richard II or some other suitably remote monarch it was indeed an indisputable right to practise archery in Petty Cury. The story went – and I heard it several times – that some undergraduates had discovered this right and then, with the appropriate equipment and clothes, had proceeded to hold up the traffic in Petty Cury (then a carriageway) while they exercised it. The story concluded that it had been necessary to repeal the right by Act of Parliament.

A similar belief, which I have again heard from many sources, is that one is allowed to relieve oneself against the rear nearside wheel of a horsedrawn vehicle. The story continued that this law was held, in the High Court, to allow a motorist to use the wheel of his vehicle for the same purpose. Or, variantly, he is 'got' on the point of law that he was using the wrong wheel.

A story still current, and on the same theme, concerns the change from horse to motor-cabs. Plying for hire is hedged about with rules, and in the old days cab-drivers had to carry a bale of hay for the horse. This provision was not withdrawn as cabs became motorised, and a taxi-driver found himself in court for failing to provide the statutory bale of hay.

The artillery changed from horses to motors as well, and a time-and-motion man was worried to find that one of the gun-crew had nothing to do. Research revealed that, in days of yore, the unemployed man was the one who had held the horse.

The whale-tumour story
is the subject of our book, and contains many elements from the above *genres*. One of its most important characteristics, however, is that the teller should be believed; for that reason he claims personal involvement with the protagonist, an almost certain talisman for securing invulnerability.

To make sure that the story is not seen as a joke, it is often unpleasant or ghastly, as witness many of the examples in this book.

To make sure that it is taken seriously it is credible, even if somewhat far-fetched; the manner of telling is such that probing the story is discouraged, as we have seen.

It may also be topical – which at once makes it suspect. In the last year or two, for example, I have heard of someone surfing when, 'Crunch!' a shark takes a bite out of his 'solid fibreglass surf-board'. After a time, I heard of incidents of the shark *slicing the surf-board in half*. It takes little imagination to guess the parentage of that one.

Since timeliness can play an important part in the fashioning of a WTS, it is not unusual to find the WTSs of yesterday becoming the jokes of today, as understanding spreads. When the electrical telegraph was striding across the country, one old couple in particular observed the activities of the linesmen and took a keen interest in the idea that the wires could be used to transmit messages. So at Christmas they bought a pair of boots for their son who was in the big city, fastened his address and a seasonal message to them, and hung them on the telegraph pole outside their cottage. They were delighted the next day to find the boots gone and a message fastened to the pole: 'Dear Mum and Dad, thanks for the boots, just what I wanted, Merry Christmas to you both, love Jack.'

As I have said, the WTS has to be distinguished from a joke whose purpose is to amuse the listener, and for this reason, its core has to be anything but funny, and is often downright unpleasant. I say 'the core' because there are certainly many which do raise a laugh, but whenever this happens, it does not detract from the apparent truth of the story.

Often, the humour of the WTS is the humour of relief. My Grandfather told of an incident (incident – there's a word for you) in the trenches in the First World War when a brother officer clambered up in the wrong place and

> was cut in half with a burst of machine-gun fire. His top half fell down, and the legs remained standing for a time before they, too, toppled over.

My Grandfather's reaction was to laugh.

This is nothing like the laughter of humour, however. It is compounded of ... Horror? Relief that it didn't happen to you? And if you didn't laugh, what *would* you do?

Serendipity has always played an important part in my research, and when I first wrote the above words, I immediately came across a passage in *Radio Times* (73), an account by Stanley Reynolds of his hearing, as a young infantryman in Texas, a black prison-gang singing a work song.

> The scene, the beauty of their singing, of these black men who were the grandsons or great grandsons of kidnapped African men and women, the still slave descendants of slaves, burned our eyes. Someone would have to make a joke, or it would not be bearable.

So does Bottom say (MND III.1):

> I will walk up and down here, and I will sing, that they shall hear that I am not afraid.

It is whistling in the dark.

We can share our tears as we can share our laughter. When someone dies we can reduce our grief by sharing it – there is an indescribably pleasurable pain in breaking the news to others. Is it that we are gaining attention for ourselves by being the bearers of sad tidings? Certainly there is some element of reflected glory in telling some anecdote of the deceased – *de mortuis nil nisi bonum*, and the banal and the trivial assume an inflated importance until our memory of the departed comes into perspective, and the anecdotes sink back into their triviality. There is no doubt that people closely connected with bad news tend to share it with anyone at hand, including those who have little interest (a 'head-dropper', for that is their reaction), and that equally those less closely connected with it may tighten their assumed connections.

Whilst on the subject of sharing grief, it is worth pointing out that in the world of the movies, the weepie (not to mention the horror) has as strong a place as the comic.

If you care to think on, you might wonder why, if the X-film is denounced as likely to incite violence and to deprave, the comic film is not denounced as likely to incite people to treat the serious business of life with levity, and to bring into question the gravity of the church, the law, the civil service, parliament and so on. If anyone thinks that the vulgar literature, sports and pastimes of today are likely to deprave, corrupt and incite violence, he had better take a look at those of yesteryear.

When Vic Matthews took over Beaverbrook Newspapers, and stated that he 'wanted to talk about the good things that are being done', I remembered the newspaper in the U.S. which printed only good news. It went out of business – which will go first, the policy or the papers? People like bad news, and it travels faster than good – how soon after the event did you hear of the assassination of JFK?

The conventions of politeness allow the WTS to survive. If we were brutally honest (and perhaps if we know the teller well enough, we are) we would say: 'Come off it, I heard that last week/years ago, and it didn't happen in Troon/Llantwit Major, it happened in Market Harborough/Bootle to a friend of *mine*. Sometimes, the anaesthetic of the teller's claiming the story to be true robs us of all memory of having heard it before. I have certainly noticed myself taking a different attitude to anecdotal conversation since I started collecting WTSs, and those who have discussed the work have remarked the same thing.

So unless one has the right relationship with someone, it is not possible to laugh in his face and call his veracity into question. And the affectation of kinship with the protagonist of the story both lends verisimilitude to an otherwise bald and unconvincing narrative, and protects the teller.

In a short story (3), Isaac Asimov suggests that sense of humour was bestowed on the race by extraterrestrial watchers.

The gift, it was alleged, was a control in a giant experiment – jokes were introduced by the experimenters, and as long as the subjects kept laughing, it was known that they hadn't rumbled that they were being observed. One day, it was realized that jokes were never seen in creation, laughter stopped, so did the experiment. Convoluted.

The late Dudley Clews (mathematician and cornettist) decided to invent a joke, tell it to someone at Land's End, and catch it when it arrived at John O'Groats. But inventing a new joke, with the uniqueness necessary for this experiment, is far from easy. It came to him very early in the morning, and, with that adrenal excitement which accompanies such invention, he had to rush out and tell someone. He banged on a neighbour's door, and the victim, unaware of the privilege which was being bestowed on him, listened blearily and unwillingly to Dudley's story. At the end, Dudley waited expectantly for the deserved acclaim. All he got was: 'Piss off, you daft bugger, you made it up!' (Slam)

The really interesting thing would be to know what the story was, but to my lasting regret, I never found out.

One of the features of stories told and retold is that they become embroidered and intermingled.

Embroidery of stories can take place on several levels. At its simplest, it is the 'friend' to whom it happened, when in fact it was a 'foaf'. By claiming the friendship, the tellers draws his tale one step nearer to reality. The next stage of broderie is to name the friend, or at least to identify him as 'a chap I used to work with'. On the same plane, I think, is to name the place at which the incident happened – and this will have to suit the teller, such as: 'When I was in Truro a couple of years ago.'

As we progress up the stages of broderie, the tale itself becomes modified, new heights of nast being added according, as I've said, to the teller and his audience. And the thought can become the deed.

Suppose you think: 'One day, I'm going to put a grinning, maniacal mask on the back of my head, go for a drive, lean out of the window when I overtake someone, and give him a fright.' The idea is neither brilliant nor novel; Harpo Marx performs a variant of it in *Monkey Business*, and I first heard of a foaf doing it in the early fifties. However, that is the basis of the idea, but the imaginative teller sees some difficulty in frightening an overtakee because of the geometry of the manoeuvre, so he uses a *left-hand drive car*. Having got thus far, the frightened overtakee can do one of several things – he can take the foaf's number and report him to the police, he can run into a ditch, or he can have a heart-attack. The prankster may use a gorilla mask (something to do with *Morgan – a Suitable case for Treatment*?) and the whole incident may occur abroad (which saves the LHD car), since it is well known that abroad all roads have a sheer precipice on one side. In that case, as like as not, the victim's car bursts into flames, and he is fried.

Now, all these details I have added to the basic story may have been derived, consciously or subconsciously, from other stories, plays, films – from anywhere in my experience. When I first heard the 'finger in the door' story (p. 149), it didn't have the added refinement of the attacker being traced by the police. I took that refinement, and added it to the mask story above. When I first heard the 'headless motorcyclist' story (p. 148), it had no heart-attack in it. That was another addition which I borrowed, and grafted on to the mask story. And so on.

Enough of this. Why read menus and cookery books when you can eat the food? Read on and *bon appetit*.

1

The Whale Mistaken

> The man who never made a mistake never made anything.
>
> —Old Excuse

A mis-hearing can be completely innocuous, but it can easily lead to sulks, punches-up or even death.

An innocuous example:

Speaker: What a *bonne idée*.

Hearer: What a bonny day.

Another, recounted by George Melly (57), concerned an argument he was having with Ian Christie wherein the latter averred that George's thought patterns were the result of his 'middle-class background.' George agreed 'that this might be true, but that it was after all an accident where any of us were *dropped from the womb*.'

'Don't try and confuse the issue with that Surrealist bollock,' shouted Ian. George was puzzled and asked Ian what he found Surrealist in what he'd been saying. It turned out that Ian thought that George had said 'lopped off the moon'.

Ripley reports 'A Tragic Mistake' (74):

> In 1831, during Napoleon III's coup d'état, when an aide reported that the mob was facing the Imperial Guard, Count de St Arnaud, who was just troubled with a cough, exclaimed: 'Ma sacrée toux!' (My damned cough!) This the aide understood to mean 'massacrez tous!' (massacre everybody). The order to fire was given and thousands of human lives were lost.

If people hear, or see, something which is not there – and this is often wishful thinking – we may see the birth of a WTS. Similarly, they may *not* hear or see something which *is* there.

A foaf went up and down a street in London, asking for paw-paw – the fruit of *Asimina triloba*. At last she received the reply: 'Sorry, we don't have paw-paw, but we can let you have some Kit-e-Kat.'

The mother of a foaf is an inveterate traveller. One day, she wandered up a mountain track somewhere in Europe, and found herself at a frontier post. Naturally, she was asked to produce her 'papers'; she searched in her handbag, but found that she had left her passport behind in her hotel. On an impulse, she pulled out her Post Office Savings Book and offered it to the guard. He studied it carefully, turning over the pages. Then he looked at her. 'You. You are always visiting Ondemand. This will make a pleasant change.' He stamped the book, and handed it back to her with a smart salute.

The wife of a foaf returned from a shopping expedition to find a bottom sticking up from under the kitchen sink. 'It's about time you cleared that, you lazy sod,' she shouted, patting the protruding posterior playfully. 'I'm very sorry, madam,' said the plumber, emerging. 'Your husband telephoned me last week, but I wasn't able to come until today.'

Other versions of this hilarious happening are found. It is a caravan site. The wife returns from shopping to find her husband, wearing a shirt and nothing else, bending over the basin. Playfully she grabs a handful from behind: 'Ding, ding,' she laughs. Well, one caravan looks very like another ... (Shades of the kindly neighbour in Chapter 7).

College rooms are notoriously cold. Many years ago, a certain supervisor at Queens' hit on a way of conducting comfortable supervisions – comfortable for him, that is. He acquired an electrically-heated flying suit in which to cocoon himself, while his pupils shivered. One day, he left the suit to warm up while he went to transact some other business before the start of the supervision. He was delayed; something went wrong with the thermostat and the suit started to smoulder. The first supervisee arrived, knocked, entered, and saw what he took to be the remains of the don smouldering on the chair. Hysterically he raised the alarm – just as his supervisor returned. The student took one look at the 'ghost' and passed out cold.

Certain actors are well-known for their love of the bottle. One such met a friend of his in *The Salisbury* (St Martin's Lane) and they drank right through the lunch time. At last, our actor says that he's on in a play at the New Theatre, and why doesn't his friend come along and see it?

'Thank you very much,' he replies, and together they roll along to the Theatre, and up to the Dress Circle – where there's plenty of room. The house lights go down and the play starts. After a time our actor turns to his friend and says: 'You're going to enjoy this bit: this is where I come on.'

This same actor was on another occasion on tour with a Shakespearean company, and this time managed to appear on the stage, though again in an unworthy condition – tight as Andronicus, as they say in the trade. Off he went:

Now is the wister of our dincontest
Made glorious Yorkshire by the summer sun
And all the clous that loused upon our housed
In the deep ... the deep ... bosom ...

The audience began to murmur, and a voice shouted: 'You're pissed!'

The Duke of Gloucester (afterwards King Richard III) rolled down to the footlights and swayed glazedly at the house.

'You're quite correct,' he enunciated, 'but just wait until you see the Duke of Buckingham.'

Every age has produced its reputedly drunk actor, and the stories are much the same.

Then there was a drag artiste who used to nip around to a certain pub between shows for a pint, and one evening it was the landlady's birthday, so she asked if he'd be able to return for a drink with her after the show. 'I'll come and do you a turn, Ducky,' promises the performer, and returns to the theatre. At the end of the evening he's as good as his word, goes back to the pub and a good time is had by all until the small hours. He emerges into the street, and then the awful truth dawns: the theatre has long since been locked up, and there he is, standing in his transigear as this awful woman, trying to explain in an abnormally deep voice to a taxi-driver that he hasn't any money on him, but if he'll take him back to his flat . . .

A foaf is a consultant gynaecologist in Harley Street. One day, he received the wife of an Indian prince, who desperately wanted children but had been unsuccessful over the years of her marriage: she was visiting the foaf, she said, because she had heard that he was the best in London and, therefore, in the world. He received this news with his customary modesty, asked her many questions, took copious notes. Then he indicated a screen in the corner of the consulting-room.

'Would you go over there, please, take off all your clothes, and lie on the couch?'

'Oh no!' she wailed. 'I want an *Indian* baby.'

Very often, it is politically inopportune for certain public figures to die, and so it was, it was said, for Queen Alexandra. In order to prove that she was still alive (after her death), she was, according to legend, propped in a carriage

ALRIGHT, ALRIGHT, DON'T GO MAD!

and driven through the streets, with a cord tied to her wrist so that she could be made to wave at the crowds. Many corpses have had to behave like this.

A foaf who is a Readymix driver suspected his wife of infidelity. One day, he made sure that she thought he was going to be miles away, and then drove past his house. Sure enough, the bedroom curtains were drawn, and outside stood a brand-new Triumph convertible. Sickened at this display of opulence, our driver had a brilliant idea on the spur of the moment – he drove round the block and prepared his load of cement. Then he returned, positioned his lorry, extended the chute, reversed the barrel and filled the Triumph convertible with Readymix. As he packed up to drive away, a foxy little man came out of his house, climbed on to a bicycle, and pedalled briskly away in the opposite direction.

A foaf runs the library-book distribution service for a Northern county. One day, he had an urgent telephone call, saying that a consignment of parcels for distribution to a number of branch libraries had been hi-jacked. He couldn't understand it at all – who could these thieving bibliophiles be? The news started to come in from the police – boxes of his books were being found dumped along the East Lancs Road. Suddenly the whole thing became clear – the books were packed in reject Johnnie Walker boxes from a nearby paper-converting plant.

A lady was travelling to hospital by bus; on arrival she found that her specimen had been stolen. Why? Well, the only vessel she had been able to find was a Haig whisky bottle.

Having got that far, I was delighted to find another foaf who had left the sample in her bicycle basket: rather than steal it, the remover (said to be an American – it was during the war) had left two £1 notes as thanks.

Another foaf spent a good deal of money on some hash and whisky, sold to him by an Arab. The 'hash', however, turned out to be dried camel dung, so he was in two minds about the 'whisky'.

He could always have done as a friend of mine did – try it on someone else. This friend was told, in great glee, by an obnoxious colleague of how he had peed into a bottle of drink in order to pay someone back. Now, this obnoxious colleague had a bottle of sherry which he would produce from his usually locked filing cabinet when an important client visited. One day, my friend found the cabinet open! ... and peed into the bottle. The next important client (who happened to be an expensive woman) accepted a glass of sherry. 'Hm,' she said 'rather ... unusual.' She seemed to enjoy it. Obnoxious guessed what had happened – but took it like a man.

I am indebted to Mrs Janie Gothard for the following:

The parcel of dried fruit for the anniversary cake duly arrived from Australian cousins, with no note or letter. The ingredients, including some greyish powder – to add spice? – were duly mixed and baked, and the cake pro-nounced by family and friends as 'gorgeous'.

Then the delayed letter arrived, with the instructions: 'By the way, the grey powder in the packet is Uncle Joe's ashes. Would you please scatter them on his mother's grave?'

In the first (and slightly more credible) version I heard of that, the ashes arrived in a cocoa (or some such) tin, and were put to use, because the foafs thought that it was some new Australian brand.

The wife of a foaf was having trouble cleaning the lavatory, so she put some strong acid down it and went out shopping. The foaf returned home unexpectedly in order to use the loo somewhat violently: the acid splashed his bottom, and his wife returned to find him writhing on the floor. She immediately sized up the situation, doused her spouse liberally with water and telephoned for an ambulance. When the ambulance men were told what had happened, they laughed so much that they dropped the stretcher and the foaf broke his leg.

A foaf was not feeling well, but just couldn't see how he could miss the office Christmas party, so he took the train to town and over-indulged himself enormously, with the result that he was really very ill in several directions at once. So he stumbled into an army surplus shop on his way back to the station, asked for a pair of trousers – '38 waist, quick, here's a fiver' – the assistant stuffed them into a bag, and the foaf just managed to scramble into an empty compartment on the corridorless train back home. He removed his mucky old trousers, rolled them up, and threw them out of the window. Then he opened the bag, and found that somehow he had bought a denim jacket.

A foaf is a vet in Saudi Arabia. A friend of *his* out there was in charge of building a school: top-class stuff, no skimping. After a time, however, the cesspit filled up, and on inspection the cause was found to be lots and lots of little stones. The architect conferred with the headmaster and found that the local custom was to use stones rather than lavatory paper. The pit was cleared, and the headmaster discussed the matter with the school, explaining that with this system, one had to use paper. However, the cesspit filled up *again*. This time, each stone was found to be wrapped in a piece of paper . . .

In the village where I live, there are two main phases of building, to be joined as the village is completed. The parts are known as 'up the hill' and 'down the hill', and it is well-known to residents of each phase that those in the other indulge in continuous wife-swapping parties. This is a very interesting tale, because inquiries have revealed that similar stories circulate in many places where there is more than a certain number of (new) houses. I haven't found the critical size yet.

At a rape trial, the woman in the case stood in the witness box, and was asked what the defendant had said to her. She gulped a few times, and then whispered, 'I dare not say.' 'Write it on a piece of paper, then,' said the kindly judge. This was duly done, and the paper was passed around the court. It arrived at the jury, and passed silently along the front row, and then the back. However, it was a hot day, and one of the lady jurors had dozed off, so she was somewhat startled to feel a nudge from her male neighbour, and to be passed a piece of paper reading, 'I'm going to screw you like you've never been screwed before.' 'How dare you,' she shouted, and slapped his face.

A version of this is reported (28) where it is the male who is asleep, and, on being handed the piece of paper, hastily stuffs it into his pocket. The judge asks the usher to retrieve the 'evidence', whereupon the man says, 'Oh, no, your honour, that note is a personal matter between the lady and me.' This version is dismissed because of the unlikelihood of a male juror being asleep during the high-spot of the trial – the evidence of the girl. The former version therefore seems the more likely.

44

An elderly lady went shopping with a £5 note. She took a train to town and during the journey nodded off to sleep. When she woke, she found another old lady in the compartment, also asleep. She took out her purse to check her shopping list, and her £5 note was gone. On an impulse she looked into her companion's bag and there on top – no attempt to hide it – was the £5 note. She removed it quietly, for she had no intention of getting the old lady into trouble, and left the compartment. After her day's shopping, she was met by her husband at the station. 'However did you get all that stuff?' he asked. 'You left your £5 note on the mantelpiece.'

A story of passing examinations comes from the States (28): I haven't come across it here yet. A student has to write two essays, but can only tackle one of them, so he writes what looks like the ending of the first (the one he can't do) essay at the top of a new page, rules it off, and then does the second. The instructor doesn't like to admit that he's lost half the answer paper, and marks him on double the 'second' essay – top grade.

A variation of this is to hand in the answers you can do, take the other part of the paper away and complete it as quickly as possible, then slip it on the floor at the back of the class and wait for it to be found and handed in.

In a third variety, the examiner receives a letter 'obviously intended' for the examinee's mother, and mother appears to get the answers, which she then appears to mail to the examiner. Clearly this won't work unless you are being examined by post.

A housewife in Selly Oak went to fetch in her milk one morning, and there on the step was a shabby carry-cot containing a little coloured baby with a note pinned to the moth-eaten blanket: 'Please look after me.' Now, this lady badly wanted to adopt a child, so she took the carry-cot into the house. Just then her husband came down, took one look at it and put his foot down: 'Oh no, we're not having *that*,' and he called the police. A car arrived, and a policeman and policewoman got out and came to investigate the foundling. What had at first sight appeared to be a mattress turned out to be a pillowcase. And it was stuffed with wads of £20 notes.

A critic went to see a play, and turned in his piece the next day. The editor was far from pleased when he found that his rivals had reported the play in a rather different way, for it appeared that one of the actors had been accidentally stabbed during a duel. He called in his critic. 'How did you come to miss this story?' he thundered. The critic drew himself up to his full height. 'Sir,' he replied, 'I am the dramatic critic, not a crime reporter.'

That's just one manifestation of the incompetent reporter. In other versions, he goes to see the beginning of the play, then gets detained at the bar and misses the stabbing. In another version, he just gets detained at the bar, and misses the reality of the curtain getting stuck, or the theatre burning down, or whatever it is that happens. Sometimes it's not the dramatic critic. It may be the music critic, or the sports reporter who writes the report of the concert, or game, before it takes place, only to find that it's cancelled, or rained off. Since most games (like most pieces of music) have a score of some sort, I find it difficult to understand how this one works.

Photogravure magazines, colour supplements and the like are often printed well in advance. There is a story of a well-known magazine which prepared an account of a Hollywood wedding, but on the day it hit the streets, the divorce was announced.

There was a poor Neapolitan family, working in the north of Italy. The father died, and the family wished to return him to his native soil; however, they found that the cost of taking a coffin from north to south was far beyond their slender means. So they dressed him in his Sunday suit, and took him south by train, sitting between his two eldest sons. For some reason, both had to get out at a station, and nearly missed the train. However, they just managed to clamber on to the last carriage and fell into the gangway. They made their way along to the front carriage, and found that the old man had disappeared. There was the most terrible scene, knives flashed, and eventually the frightened family in the compartment confessed. Apparently the train had started with a jolt, and a large suitcase had fallen down on the old man who had, of course, fallen forwards on to the floor. They examined him – 'Mama mia! He's dead! And it was our suitcase ...' So they had thrown the body off the train.

A lady and her daughter were travelling on the Continent, and arrived at an hotel in Paris as their last stop on the way home to England. They retired to their separate bedrooms and the daughter, who was especially tired after supervising all the luggage, dropped off to sleep almost immediately, and did not wake until late in the morning. She rose, and went to the door which connected her room to her mother's, but found it locked – she went round by the corridor and knocked. There was no reply. She spoke to the hall porter, the assistant manager, the manager, and all told the same story; that she had arrived alone, not with her mother; the insinuation was that she must be losing her reason. They showed her the room where she alleged that her mother stayed the night, and the furniture and décor were quite different.

However, the truth is eventually unearthed – after she had gone to bed, her mother had been taken ill and called the doctor. The doctor had recognized that mother was suffering from cholera, and would surely die. Not wishing to lose all his guests and his reputation, the manager had insisted that the woman was removed from his hotel, the room was quickly redecorated and refurnished, and the whole staff sworn to secrecy.

A respectable amount of research has gone into this story, which is quoted by Briggs (10 & 11), who refers us to Woollcott (96) (for some reason referred to as 'Northcott'), and also to the film *So Long at the Fair*. Woollcott found that it was in a novel by Mrs Belloc-Lowndes (5) and in another by Lawrence Rising (76) and traced it back in various guises to the *Detroit Free Press*, 1889. Woollcott puts his finger on the essence of the WTS in referring to this one:

> For such a story to travel round the world by word of mouth, it is necessary that each teller of it must believe it true, and it is common practice for the artless teller to seek to impart that belief to his listeners by affecting kinship, or at least a lifelong intimacy, with the protagonist of the adventure related.

Just as people sometimes disappear without trace, so do they sometimes appear without parentage. There is, for example, the famous economist Milton Keynes, one of the rising young men of the 1920s. Albert and Lady Margaret Hall are a famed couple. And it was a pity to have missed the concert which was to have been given by Viola da Gamba and her harpsichord.

Parsons (55) quotes the *Nottingham Daily Express*:

> We have printed, verbatim, all that Phillimore gives on the subject. Nor has Phillimore rested his facts on Prideaux alone. He quotes Ibid as his authority for paragraphs 3 and 4, both of which paragraphs confirm paragraph 2 based on Prideaux.

I have always wanted to start a publication called *Ibid*. However, when in the RAEC in Germany, I was faced each month with having to set the Third Class Army Certificate of Education English paper. One of the obligatory questions was always a comprehension test, based on a newspaper report.

One month, I was completely unable to find a suitable paragraph so I concocted one, from a fictitious publication called *Orb and Sceptre*. How gratifying to think that a copy of this examination paper is somewhere enshrined in the BAOR archives. *Caveat lector.*

Just as bombs were reported as having been dropped at Random, so it was reported that the Germans had surrendered En Masse. And somewhere along the line, a visiting lecturer who had attended Queen's College, Oxford, and been granted an MA degree, was described reverently as 'Master of the Queen's Oxen.'

No book on WTSs would be complete without the vanishing granny, otherwise known as the stolen corpse, oft reported, in numerous guises to suit the occasion yet still (it would seem) believed to be true by both tellers and listeners.

A couple went touring in Spain, and took the wife's mother with them. While on holiday, the old lady died, and they didn't know what to do. They decided to return home at once with the body wrapped in their tent on the roof-rack. Somehow they made it through the customs, drove home as fast as possible, and went indoors for a cup of tea. When they went outside again to fetch the tent, they found that some-one had stolen the car. And after overcoming the problem of explaining to the police what had happened, they still had another hurdle to overcome – neither car nor granny has been found, and they will have to wait seven years before she can be presumed dead.

2

The Whale Entombed

I had walled the monster up within the tomb!

The Black Cat
Edgar Allan Poe

Poe knew full well that walling up things and people is guaranteed to produce a shiver – somehow we need to suspect that under the calm exterior is something hidden and macabre.

Anyone who read at a tender age, as I did, such Poe classics (67) as *The Black Cat, The Cask of Amontillado,* or *The Tell-tale Heart,* is hardly likely to forget the tales, even if as the years pass they merge into a certain sameness of plot.

For the walling up of the soul, I would refer you to a lesser-known Poe tale, *The Facts in the Case of M. Valdemar.* If I may prune the story drastically, M. Valdemar was on his deathbed, and the storyteller suddenly realized that no-one had 'as yet been mesmerized *in articulo mortis.*' So M. Valdemar became the subject of this new experiment. He remained mesmerized for about seven months, until

at length the same hideous voice, which I have already described, broke forth: 'For God's sake! – Quick! quick! – put me to sleep – or, quick! – waken me! – quick! – *I say to you that I am dead!*'

Our mesmerist of course obliges:

As I rapidly made the mesmeric passes, amid ejaculations of 'dead! dead!' absolutely *bursting* from the tongue and not from the lips of the sufferer, his whole frame at once – within the space of a single minute, or even less, shrunk – crumbled – absolutely *rotted* away beneath my hands. Upon the bed, before the whole company, there lay a liquid mass of loathsome – of detestable putrescence.

That's the end. It's done one good thing for us – provided the verb 'to *Valdemar*' which is what happens to certain instant puddings if they're left too long.

People (rightly) find a fascination in the fact that great buildings (cathedrals for example) are honeycombed with passages and rooms of which one would not dream until some concealed door is opened, revealing a glimpse of the works. Museums and art galleries display but a fraction of their possessions: behind doors through which members of the staff disappear with the aid of their jangling pass-keys are massive hoards of treasures, and innumerable offices and workshops.

Any house with servants' quarters is the same – there is an abrupt change in style and décor which tells you which side of the blankets you're on. I asked for the loo at Chatsworth, and entered, as they say about a certain London store, a whole new world.

Stories of secret passages and tunnels – or at least rumours thereof – abound wherever there is an old building. The Manor House is joined to the Church. The Monastery is joined to the Nunnery. Travelling further afield, we find that the Sphynx is a massive secret doorway to an underground system of passages leading to the several pyramids. And it should come as no surprise to find that our very planet is hollow, or at least a complex labyrinth of passages (52 *et al*).

With so much effort having been put into the construction of now-forgotten hiding places, it is natural that they should be unearthed from time to time, with attendant legends.

For example, when things which are walled up are re-discovered, they would seem to have a habit of crumbling. Usually they stay whole long enough for the discoverers to have a good look at them, and then collapse in a pile of dust.

This happened to a roundhead's hat which Charlie Ison said he found under the floor of the airing cupboard in my parents' house. For a moment it was visible in its pristine glory, as fresh as the day it had been put there. Then it crumbled.

51

And it adds to the storyteller's armoury of the marks of mystery:

Inside the chamber, close to the threshold, lay four human skeletons, a few colourful rags still attached to the bones. They were ancient. As soon as the draught hit them, they simply fell apart. They must have been lying here for many thousands of years (29).

In Fellini's *Roma*, an underground railway is being tunnelled (in Rome) and they discover a very beautiful Roman villa. It exhibits some exquisite murals which, even as they gaze upon them, dissolve and run down the walls.

Slow but inexorable, this is the fate of the cave-paintings at Lascaux and elsewhere; we may brood on this as the very epitome of self-destructive art.

In that great pile which is the University of Manchester Institute of Science and Technology, there is said to be a lavatory built specially for Queen Victoria in case she wanted to open her bowels as well as the building. The lava-

tory is now walled up (I'm told). Whether or not she used it is unrecorded. And whether it was walled up because it was too inconvenient a convenience, or because it was considered too reginal for ordinary use I don't know either.

Another story of Queen Victoria's movements avers that she was not in favour of lavatories on trains. It was therefore necessary to ensure that there was a supply of suitably-spaced halts along the route of any royal progress. That is why Milton Keynes is where it is – before the railway age there was hardly anything there: then Queen Victoria wished to visit the West country, and a station had to be built at Woburn Sands; hence Milton Keynes. That's what I've heard, anyway.

Mysteries, mysteries. According to a reviewer, a recent book on the Marquis de Sade states that the British Library contains unpublished de Sade manuscripts, 'only to be read in the presence of the Archbishop of Canterbury and two other trustees.' (In fact, that's the publisher's blurb.) In response to the reviewer's inquiry, the keepers at the British Library have given their official assurance that no such manuscripts exist. But we all 'know' that there are such holdings in large libraries – indeed, the tower of the Cambridge University Library is, according to a tradition which cannot be very old (for the building is about my age), 'full of pornography.'

Similarly, I suppose we should classify Joanna Southcott's Box. The Panacea Society is always advertising for the Bishops to get together and open the Box. I don't understand why the Bishops don't call the bluff of the Panacea Society – it would make a lighthearted entertainment at an ecclesiastical conference. If the box were found to contain our salvation, the divines would presumably be able to congratulate themselves on their wisdom. If it contained some fatuity, they could all have a good laugh. In either case, the Panacea Society would be saved the expense of all that advertising.

In 1945, Dr Ingram of the Low Temperature Research Institute, came to talk to our Science Club at school about the possibility of preserving food by freezing – we were cautious, then delighted, as we sampled strawberries which had been picked before the war. Today, we see no wonder in such things; we merely grumble if the shop has run out of some frozen delicacy, and insure our home freezers against power cuts. For our WTS, we have to turn to more exotic sources, the most well-known of which is of course Siberia, where Russian scientists find mammoths preserved in blocks of ice, hack them out, and eat them. And everyone knows as well that tins of food from Scott's expedition were as fit to eat when they were recovered as they had been when they were buried.

These occurrences are not inexplicable, nor yet unbelievable, based as they are on well-tried principles. But what about the pyramids? (What about them?) As anyone with a quarter of an eye for the appropriate sections of bookshops will know, there is tremendous power of some sort which is concentrated by pyramids, and makes people feel more at peace, better able to meditate, get a better night's sleep, etc. I tried hanging a cardboard pyramid over the bed, but the string broke and it woke us.

It is not clear which is the cause and which the effect. Can it be that the pyramids of Egypt are nothing more than power concentrators of some sort? Or is it merely a by-product of a shape hit upon by chance, a shape clean-cut and easy to build, which will last for a very long time indeed? Is the power a by-product of the pyramid? We're working on it. Suffice it to say that the power may have given rise to two WTSs, or vice versa.

First, grains of wheat which were put into the pyramids of Egypt thousands of years ago were said to have germinated instantly when given the right conditions.

Second is the model said to have been found inside the Great Pyramid, a model representing a landscape with rivers of quicksilver (lovely alchemical name) running through it. And the rivers had been running for centuries. Pyramid power? Perpetual motion? M. C. Escher? Where is the model now?

The idea of drowned cities – whether in volcanic ash (Pompeii) or water – is one to take the fancy, and what more expected than to find stories of their continuing to function in some ghostly way?

Take a day's journey by boat from Cromer to Harwich, and what is the most striking scene that the coast presents to the astonished gaze? Here and there a steeple-top projects out of the waters: it is all that is left of a once-flourishing little town now buried beneath the swirling tides which are rapidly beating down the cliffs, and year by year getting a little further inland. Cromer, overlooking the sea, and protected by a double breakwater which in time of storm is insufficient to keep the raving waves in check, was once four miles from the coast, and the old town of Shipden lies beneath the sea. The legend runs that as you stand on the crumbling cliffs you can hear the sweet faint sound of bells rising from the sea depths, and that if you look intently at low tide you can see the shadowy outlines of the whelmed houses which made the Cromer of Centuries ago ... (90)

I understood that it was the bells of Dunwich which could be heard, but our source does not mention them, though it is at pains to list the dates of disappearance of the several churches. Certainly, if by some miracle the belfry managed to remain intact such that the bells could swing under water, we should be able to hear them. But that Neptune would so order the waters as to practise change-ringing, I doubt. It is, however, a common story, and not confined to this country: Debussy's *La Cathédrale Angloutille* tells of a similar happening.

Any moment now, I expect to hear tales of the bells of Imber, that deserted village usurped by the army on Salisbury plain, the memory of which tends to make some of us change colour.

But enough of the inanimate. If we turn to the animal kingdom, and climb the evolutionary tree, we find WTSs of the walled-up along every branch.

Some years ago, tall, bouffant, lacquered hairstyles were all the rage (for women, that is). One girl decided after some months that she'd go and have her hair taken down and cleaned. As the operation proceeded, the hairdresser found that the arrangement was full of maggots. This was first told

55

to me by the brother of the hairdresser to whom it happened. Again, it may have been true, but it happened to a lot of people at the same time. Some people had black widow spiders – 'in the midst of life', etc. Others – and all must have had peculiarly insensitive scalps – had nests of mice, though I understand that this was a purposefully exotic effect sported by certain ladies at the pre-revolutionary French court – the Dame Ednas of Versailles, perhaps. Certainly, with Queen Elizabeth (the first) taking a bath once a year 'whether she needed it or not' being the height of luxury, it is clear that there have been long periods of history when it didn't need exotic hairstyles to shelter wriggling fauna.

Now that coal is out of fashion, and too precious to be kept in the bath (another WTS, *en passant*), people are generally cleaner, and their hair is not so high, in any sense. So the creepy-crawlies have been turned to the 'buy British' campaign in the following way.

A lady foaf went to the doctor with an abdominal rash. 'Aha!' said the wise medic. 'Have you bought a new skirt recently?' The patient said she had. 'Then I should go home and examine it very carefully', said the doctor, who must have felt rather like Conan Doyle on a good day. So the patient returned home, and examined the garment carefully. She noticed some irregularities in the waist-band. Curious, she started to unpick it, and found that it was 'full of lice'. The skirt, of course, had been made somewhere in the Far East.

A peculiar state of affairs obtains with the story of Robert the Bruce. I remember quite clearly being told this story at the age of nine – RtB was hiding from his enemies in a cave, and whilst in there had plenty of time to reflect on his plight. He also had plenty of time to observe a spider which appeared to be having difficulty in spinning a web. However, with great tenacity the cack-footed arachnid carried on and finally succeeded in constructing its web. RtB was thus inspired, and emerged and led his people to victory.

Many years later, thirty perhaps, I told my wife this story. Don't ask me how we got round to that. But she was surprised because her version was that RtB had been hiding in the cave, and a spider had woven a web across the entrance. Seeing the web, the pursuers assumed that nobody could be in the cave, and therefore went away; after a decent interval RtB emerged and led his people to victory. We could see no reason why both versions were not tenable, and of course they are. Most people to whom I have put the choice agree with my wife's version. Presumably there are my fellows of the class of '42, and others who came under the same tutelage, who go along with my version. Neither DNB (26) not Eyre-Todd (32) gives either version.

Let us now move from the arthropods to the vertebrates – reptilia for a start. Many of these, notably snakes, crocodiles and toads, exhibit reputed turn-off characteristics which prevent many people from getting to know them better.

Snakes have been known to jump from the ground and penetrate passing maidens – see Chapter 3. It's never happened to any foaf of mine, however, but with the release of the film *Shivers* (X) it may only be a matter of time. Not sure if I know anyone who would go and see *Shivers*, except by accident.

Alligators are a more recent subject of WTS. It seems that it was fashionable to keep pet alligators in New York, so many ladies did. And when their loved pets became too unruly, why, they just flushed them down the lavatory. So it is that the sewers of New York are teeming with enormous alligators, much to the consternation of the sewermen. It could be that, with the dependence of a great city on its sewerage system, the alligators are the reason for its recent grinding to a halt.

But the story is a variant of one of some antiquity, told by Henry Mayhew (56):

> There is a strange tale in existence among the shore-workers, of a race of wild hogs inhabiting the sewers in the neighbourhood of Hampstead. The story runs, that a sow in young, by some accident got down the sewer through an opening, and, wandering away from the spot, littered and reared her offspring in the drain; feeding on the offal and garbage washed into it continually. Here, it

is alleged, the breed multiplied exceedingly, and have become almost as ferocious as they are numerous. This story, apocryphal as it may seem, has nevertheless its believers, and it is ingeniously argued, that the reason why none of the subterranean animals have been able to make their way to the light of a day, is that they could only do so by reaching the mouth of the sewer at the river-side, while, in order to arrive at that point, they must necessarily encounter the Fleet ditch, which runs towards the river with great rapidity, and as it is the obstinate nature of a pig to swim *against* the stream, the wild hogs of the sewers invariably work their way back to their original quarters, and are thus never to be seen. What seems strange in the matter is, that the inhabitants of Hampstead never have been known to see any of these animals pass beneath the gratings, nor to have been disturbed by their gruntings.

The sewer-hunters, of whom Mayhew was writing, had never seen the wild hogs either. But rats ... that's another story. Let us return to reptiles.

> I'd rather soar to death's abode
> On eagle's wings, than 'live a toad'
>   Pent in a block of granite.
> – *Chigwell Revisited*
>   James Smith (1775–1839)

The number of toads which have crouched patiently in rocks or tree-trunks for goodness knows how long until someone wielding the appropriate tool in the appropriate place strikes the sarcophagus is legion. According to the WTS, the tomb splits, revealing the toad, which then usually 'blinks at the unaccustomed light, and hops slowly away'.

This is an old tale, since experiments to disprove it were carried out at least two centuries ago. But it still lives. Bergen Evans (30) puts it in a nutshell:

> The toad's clammy, corpselike feeling, with its suggestion that it is already dead and hence not subject to mortality, may be the basis for many stories that one hears of a toad's being liberated from the centre of a block of stone or concrete in which he had obviously lived for years, or even centuries, without nourishment or air. In the classic

version – one often sees it in the paper, date-lined from some place inaccessible to inquiry – the creature is at first seemingly lifeless. But he revives in the open air, and, to the astonishment of the excavator, hops away apparently none the worse for his strange experience. Unfortunately for the veracity of the anecdotes, a toad must have air to survive; and even with all the air, food and water that he can desire, he will not survive many years.

Robert L. Ripley, whose credulity may have been expediently tuned to his pocket, reported thus (74):

Old Rip, The Horned Toad
In the lobby of the new court house in Eastland, Texas, may be found the remains of 'Old Rip', a horned toad that lived without food or water for thirty-one years. Mr W. M. Wood of Eastland placed the toad in the corner-stone of the court house in 1897 and took it out alive on 17th February, 1928. Old Rip was alive until January 1930, when he died of pneumonia.

For a possible *modus operandi*, consult Bel and the Dragon (7).

As for the scientific experiments, it is reported (2) that Dr William Buckland (1784–1856) built an apparatus comprising 24 stone cells covered with glass panels. 12 of the cells were $12'' \times 5''$ and were of coarse oolitic limestone; 12 were $6'' \times 5''$ and of compact silaceous sandstone. Dr B. then took 12 large and 12 small toads, and put 6 of each into the cavities, then buried the whole thing in 3 feet of earth. Within 13 months, all the toads in the sandstone and the 6 small toads in the limestone were dead. The large toads in the limestone died within the next year. So there!

Moving on to mammals, we find that rats (which have the foresight to desert ships destined to sink) are now available which can live in the refrigerated containers used for shipping food. Natural selection has produced a breed of superrat, with thick fur, which can withstand arctic climes to its obvious advantage.

To cats, especially black ones, of course. In December, 1976, two cats were reported to have emerged from a frozen meat container at Peterborough, putting the countryside on red alert because of the danger of rabies. The cats had been laid out, presumed dead, and had disconcertingly risen up and run away. Their colour is unrecorded.

In the days when locomotives had fireboxes, there was a news item from time to time wherein a driver who had taken the Flying Scotsman (or some other such long-distance runner) to London had heard an untraceable mewing throughout the journey. When he arrived, he was able to track down the elusive feline and to his astonishment had found that it had travelled all the way *inside the firebox*. I heard a variant, which stated that the animal had travelled the distance *on the connecting rod*. It was always a black kitten. For a plausible story of a long-distance black kitten, consult Driver Earl (27).

Black kittens suffer the most amazing adventures. They emerge from spin-dryers or washing machines 'somewhat bedraggled, but apparently none the worse for their unusual experience'. They spend weeks in refrigerators while their owners are on holiday. And, of course, they get walled up. In that strange little film, *The Plank*, a kitten is nailed under the floor (and let out, let me hasten to add). Brian Rix avers that his cat was unwittingly cemented under the stairs when he moved house, and there were still builders at large.

One wasn't so lucky. A foaf had a cat which, attracted by the sweet smell of the Sunday joint, climbed into the (electric) oven for a feast and was shut in. When the door was opened, there was the crisp, well-cooked body of the cat.

Allow me an ornithological diversion, before I return to man himself.

A foaf moved into a new house, accompanied by an army of artisans – carpets were laid, furniture moved in and placed: it all went like a military operation. Not surprising, as the man was a retired staff officer. Precisely at 5.30, knocking-off time, the last pieces of furniture were placed, and the men went away. The family sat in the living-room, stretching their legs, congratulating themselves on their perfect arrangements. It was slightly chilly, so mother went to shut the door, and found that there was a lump under the carpet. However, they hammered it flat, and the door gave no further trouble. Then they discovered that the budgerigar was missing . . .

"GOOD JOB HE WAS WEARING HIS LITTLE BELL!"

When this is told, according to the teller and the hearer, the reaction may range from peals of laughter to floods of tears. Aficionados of the WTS, however, just say, 'Have you got the one about the budgie under the carpet?', with the reply: 'Yes, I've heard that in Edinburgh, Frinton and Hythe, sometimes it's a canary, sometimes it's a mouse and doesn't come to light until someone notices a patch of blood on the carpet.' The budgie under the carpet has even turned up in a radio quiz: what would you do if . . .?

And so to *Homo Sapiens*.

I had often heard that the Boulder Dam was full of the bodies of men of whom the Mafia had wished to dispose. It was therefore interesting to find that, when the construction of motorways started, and people could see the pouring of millions of tons of concrete going on around them, the story was soon abroad that luckless workmen were always falling into the shuttering and being lost.

The stories were often embellished by mention of sophisticated X-ray equipment which had allegedly been used (always in vain) to locate the bodies. It was seldom stated whether the workmen found their way into the concrete by accident or design; and although the stories were said to stem from eye-witness accounts, none of the eye-witnesses had, curiously enough, ever attempted to rescue their colleagues.

There can be no doubt that there is little substance in these tales, which perhaps arose when workers for some reason failed to report for duty. Similar tales have cropped up in many other countries – in the U.S.A., for example, it is popularly supposed that the victims of Mafia executions [just as I thought] are disposed of by being entombed in concrete river-piers. When accidents have occurred on construction sites, strenuous efforts have been made to rescue survivors and recover bodies – as in the case of a bridge collapse at Pasadena, California, on 17th October, 1972, when a body was actually recovered from a 100-ton block of cement, and it is very unlikely that any genuine suspicion that a worker had fallen into a mass of concrete would go unheeded (2).

Yes, I suppose so, if there was a suspicion. One cannot help feeling that many people do disappear, and nobody knows where or why. Ask the Sally Army.

Stories of people in walls are of great antiquity. Possibly the earliest, and certainly the grandest, is that ordered by the Chinese Emperor Chin Shi Huang-ti (246–210 BC), builder of the Great Wall. More than 1,000,000 coolies were buried in the 1500-mile-long structure 'to make it strong ... And he climaxed a reign of lifelong excesses and cruelty by ordering all his family and kin interred with him alive – after his death' (75).
And how about this one? (74)

In 1569, Geronimo, an Arab living in the city of Algiers, renounced Mohammedanism and publicly professed his conversion to Christianity. The infuriated rulers of Algiers thereupon placed him on the 'Fort of 24 Hours', which was then in the process of construction, and poured cement about him which entombed him within the masonry of the fort.

The slave-monk Haedo, who was Geronimo's teacher, was liberated in 1612, and promptly published a history of Geronimo's martyrdom. When the French conquered Algiers in 1830, Haedo's book was referred to, and under its guidance the actual block within which Geronimo had been immured 250 years previously was located and they removed the remains of the martyr.

Geronimo was canonised by the Catholic Church.

In another place (75), Ripley says:

Khan Jahan ordered his body interred in a tomb with his right hand protruding from its wall – and for forty years every person who visited the spot shook hands with the dead man.

I wonder what happened then?

I will end with a WTS, as told to me by Hugo Davenport.

Some years ago, the father of a friend of mine bought a fairly enormous house in the middle of Bodmin Moor, a sort of Georgian/Regency house built on the site of an older farmhouse.

In the capacious cellars they found half a dozen very large barrels. 'Oh, good!' said mother. 'We can cut them in half and plant orange trees in them.'

So they set to work to cut the barrels in half, but they found that one of them was not empty, so they set it up and borrowed the necessary equipment from the local pub. The cellar filled with a rich, heady Jamaican odour.

'Rum, by God!' said the father. It was indeed, so they decided to take advantage of some fifty gallons of the stuff before cutting the barrel in half.

About a year later, after gallons of rum punch, flip and butter had been consumed, it was getting hard to get any more rum out of the barrel, even by tipping it up with wedges. So they cut it in half, and in it found the well-preserved body of a man.

People who died in the colonies and had expressed a wish to be buried at home were shipped back in spirits, which was much more effective than brine.

Rum was pretty cheap in Jamaica, and Lord Nelson himself was sent back in brandy, as befitted a national hero.

3

Dr Whale

'Doctor, Doctor ... people keep ignoring me.'
'Next, please'.

—Old Phobia

There is a magical rapport called the doctor-patient relationship whose erosion, ascribable variously to the war, the
NHS and writers who lift the lid off the medical profession,
has been apparent for some time.

An industrial psychologist friend of mine, who has made a
special study of doctors' interviewing techniques, found himself lecturing jointly on the subject with a top surgeon of the
old school. They got together before the meeting for the
purpose of comparing notes on what each was going to say.
After the introductions, the surgeon blasted my friend: 'You
know, the whole trouble is that these days the patients don't
call you "Sir" any more.' After that, there was little more to
be said.

The same friend was on another occasion being shown
some work which was being done on the computer interviewing of patients. The computer types a question, the
patient types the answer. 'Don't you think,' my friend asked
tentatively, 'that the human element is missing from the
system?' 'Not at all,' replied the proud progenitor, 'we pro-
gram the computer to make suitably encouraging remarks
from time to time.'

The doctor-patient relationship is ticklish; the secret of
being a patient is to start in a thoroughly one-down position
(70) and gradually find out how far the doctor will let you
go. I was once referred to a specialist and, before visiting him,
looked him up in the Medical Directory so that I should
know what sort of man to expect. The Directory told me of
some interesting-looking papers he had written, so I went

66

and looked them up. Although I didn't mean to, I let on far too early in our consultation that I knew something about him. Instead of his being flattered, the information completely upset the DPR, and nothing came from the referral.

When I was a boy, medicine was simple. You had spots – it was measles. You had a cough – it was whooping-cough. And so on. There was nothing to suggest that there were more complex conditions.

If you were 'off colour', it was the liver – you were said to be 'liverish'. So my grandfather said, anyway. And his cure? A 'dose of physic'. My father's grandmother's cure was 'a good dose of cascara'. When she died, she left an enormous cupboard of Casacara Sagrada bottles – empty and full. It was great fun, because the tablets burnt like little fireworks.

Words such as 'cancer' and 'impetigo' were never spoken – it was years before I heard them. And for me at any rate, the discovery of such conditions coincided with the awakening conscience that the medical profession was not infallible.

Of course, I may have been put off doctors by our family GP who sought to cheer me up when I was a yowling infant by pretending to bash himself on the head with a mallet.

Be that as it may, it is more likely that, as I've hinted, the medical practitioner has been exposed as an ordinary human who has been through some course of training which happened to be medical. As one's experience widens, one begins to understand the extraordinary ambiguity in 'caring' – the patient must be treated as an individual human being, and yet the doctor or nurse must know exactly when caring stops and emotional involvement begins. Caring without emotional involvement is in itself an emotional strain: no wonder there are high jinks off duty.

At the same time, medical stories have swung from the perfect nurse who marries the almost-numinous doctor, and the Marcus Welbys of this world (*are* they of this world?) to Richard Gordon's more believable creations, and the M.A.S.H. team. There are endless WTSs in the medical profession, and it may be that through the exertions of these media some of them have crept out. The collection here is not wholly of that genre; it contains other stories with strong medical connections, and some which may have crossed the border from WTS to old wives' tale.

*   *   *

Current horrors, revived by books about them, are the fear of spontaneous combustion (42) and the fear of being buried alive (91).

Spontaneous combustion is 'a curious belief that had considerable currency in the days of the temperance crusades' (30) and is apparently still held by at least one person. Michael Harrison presents us with a collection of accounts of incidents ranging from those to be found in fiction (25 & 55), via those which are said to have occurred in previous centuries, to those which are said to have occurred in our own times.

He makes us think. He asks: 'what is the common factor linking three deaths on 7th April, 1938: those of John Greely, helmsman of the SS *Ulrich*; George Turner, a lorry-driver who died at Upton; and William ten Bruik who burned to death at Ubbergen in Holland?' And the answer could be that *Ulrich*, Upton and Ubbergen all begin with U.

In investigating the Phenomenon, Mr Harrison invokes Photography, Probability, Poltergeists and Pi, not to mention Phlogiston, the Pull of gravity and a Professor of Pathology. (He does not mention this alliterative connection, however.) I recommend this book, if only that the reading of it may enable you to judge better for yourself whether there is such a phenomenon as spontaneous combustion in humans as described. I would point out, however, that the Office of Population Censuses and Surveys knows nothing of spontaneous combustion, though this ignorance is no doubt 'all part of the plot.'

And the authoritative Glaister (36) shows us a photograph depicting 'Almost complete destruction of body with relatively slight surrounding damage. The fuel was supplied by the natural body fat.'

There has always been a recognition of the danger of being buried alive, and there are plenty of patents for coffins with breathing tubes, communications systems and provision for supplies of food and water pending exhumation. I would be very glad to report that live burial is just not on, but unfortunately Glaister (36) is far from reassuring:

There have been a number of cases in recent years when bodies of people who have been examined by qualified medical practitioners, sometimes in hospitals, have been transported to mortuaries where they have been found to be alive by the mortuary attendants. *This gives the profession a bad image and should be avoided.*

The italics are mine, for it is not made clear which profession is meant. One would like to think that it's the qualified medical practitioner, but I fear that the implication is that mortuary attendants ought to stand by with clubs at the ready rather than drawing attention to the faulty diagnoses of their more highly-esteemed brethren.

Still in the mortuary, one of the great forensic pathologists was (naturally enough) a frequent visitor to a certain London mortuary, which was always immaculately kept by one of the old school of attendants bursting with pride at his calling. There arose between the pathologist and the attendant that brand of friendship which cements two such men of relative standing – officer and batman, tycoon and chauffeur, etc. 'Your mortuary is so clean that you could eat off the floor', oft quipped the pathologist.

One particularly heavy day, the pathologist returned

from Bristol to find a message at Paddington station calling him to an urgent case at the mortuary, so he bought some sandwiches and a pie at the buffet and took a taxi to the mortuary. He rushed in, case and umbrella in one hand, half-eaten pie in the other. The attendant came to take his coat and in the scramble the pie fell to the floor. The pathologist looked at the attendant, and the attendant looked at the pathologist. The pathologist gulped, and picked up the pie. 'Well,' he said, 'here goes . . .'

Death is a peculiar subject. As I have remarked elsewhere, to have known a recently deceased person, however slightly, confers some reflected glory on us. If we knew the deceased more intimately, it takes some time to come to terms with the fact that we shall never see, nor hear, him again. Some never come to terms with the fact, and are useful fodder for some mediums and purveyors of religion. Not all, though. I doubt if anyone would dispute that the roots of primitive religion may lie in the mysticism of death. We have neither the room nor the brief to explore such thoughts here, but the following quotation brings us back to the WTS, and demonstrates what one might call the Pelion-Ossa syndrome – the more a person's statement is questioned, the more is he likely to wind himself deeper and deeper into the mud of unjustified defence.

That the human body changes weight at the moment of death is believed by great numbers of people who, however, divide themselves into opposing camps – the lighter-weights and the heavier-weights.

Those who believe that the body becomes lighter seem to think that the soul has weight, weight that must of necessity depart with it, and – with that brisk regard of strict veracity which so frequently marks discussions of this nature – have claimed that dying men, at the very moment of their decease, have been placed on delicate scales that have recorded their mortuary degravitation. But these persons have never been able to specify in just what ghoulish laboratory this took place, or what private home was so interestingly equipped, or the names and addresses of the relatives who so commendably placed scientific and religious curiosity before sentimental concern for the patient's comfort . . .

More prevalent is the other belief, expressed in the phrase 'dead weight', that a body weighs more after death. But it only seems to weigh more . . . (30)

From death to birth. At the time of the emergence of the pill, there were numerous stories of daughters removing their mothers' pills for their own use, and substituting something similar in appearance. Presumably this was before the days of the bubble-pack. The mother, of course, became pregnant, and the daughter didn't.

A foaf's sister shares a flat with two other girls. She told of their inebriated return one night, with three young men. Her older sharer – more experienced – asked the younger if she'd like a contraceptive device, an offer eagerly accepted. In the morning, the donee was asked how she got on with it. 'All right,' she said, 'except that it tasted horrible.'

This puts one in mind of the newly-qualified lad who

issued an unsophisticate with some suppositories, instructing him to insert one in the rectum each morning and evening. When the patient returned it was clear that he hadn't followed the instructions – *'Have* you been inserting them in your rectum?' 'Course I have Doctor. What d'you expect me to do, stick them up my bloody arse?'

A young friend of mine was completely nonplussed when the doctor handed him an ice-cream carton, saying 'Make me a stool.'

There is no virtue in obscurity for the sake of delicacy.

There are tales of precocious little children, who, desirous of the company of a little co-sibling, pierce the french letter pack with a needle, an attack which of course passes unnoticed in the heat of the moment of use.

These little activities doubtless gave rise to the expected result of a sperm-ovum union, but we should spend some time considering more far-fetched myths of sterility, impregnation, telegony and parturition.

Sterility, caused by agents at a distance using secret means, is unpleasant to contemplate and difficult to prove or disprove. It has recently been officially stated that the Russians have *not* been using beams of microwave energy to sterilize the inhabitants of the American Embassy. But whoever thought that they had been? My guess is that if radio and television were not (on balance) a boon and a blessing to men, the electromagnetic radiation which enables them to function would be accused of causing any dread disease or condition for which a scapegoat was needed.

That the skill of the chef could be endangered by the development of the frozen pre-packed meal and the microwave oven is perhaps rationalized and articulated in current microwave oven myths: that your kidneys can be cooked, that they make you sterile, and that chefs are issued with 'Geiger counters' to measure the dose of radiation they receive (21). And as soon as someone asserts that he knows someone whose kidneys *have* been cooked, etc., there is your WTS.

Of course, 'cooking kidneys' can be a joke on a par with

making things out of one's own head, or asking a butcher if he has any brains. But I think that there is slightly more depth in the kidneys being singled out by the death-rays for cooking. My mother averred that if you sat on radiators, you would 'melt the fat round your kidneys,' backing up the story by saying that there were people at school to whom it happened. Of all the internal organs, the ones with which most people are familiar are the kidneys – they are much more defined than the amorphous liver. Again, 'kidneys' is a euphemism for 'testicles', and that, added to the urinogenital connection, gives the kidneys a special aura of singularity, and links kidneys and sterility.

Geiger counters are, of course, for detecting radioactivity (which might make you sterile) and not microwave radiation. This particular story (the carrying of Geiger counters) has actually appeared in the national press. As if chefs didn't have a hard enough life slaving over hot stoves without having to lug pieces of monitoring equipment about. Most of them would probably settle for sterility. The germ of the idea probably springs from the dosemeters which radiographers and others wear.

However, the history of insidious sterility should give us no cause for complacency. The pioneers of X-rays and radioactivity at the turn of the century had no idea what their work was doing to them until it was too late.

Perhaps it was not surprising to find that:

In the summer of 1943 absenteeism among woman war workers [in the U.S.A.] reached such proportions that sabotage was suspected and agents of the FBI were called in to investigate. Their finding, confirmed by other governments and private agencies, was that women were being driven from lathes and benches by strange sexual fears. Some feared sterility from welding or from working with ultra-violet or infra-red rays. Some feared that riveting caused cancer of the breast. A wholly new and fictitious female disorder – 'riveter's ovaries' – had been invented. And scores of women engaged in filling fire-extinguishers for aeroplanes had left in panic when it was rumoured that the material they were handling, carbon tetra-chloride, caused pregnancy. (30)

73

. Mind you, there's nothing to say that these rumours were not started by saboteurs. As for the last one, that CCl_4 causes pregnancy, what more evidence is needed for the necessity of a proper sex education?

The causes of pregnancy (apart from the well-known one) are many and varied. One of the most persistent is that women have conceived after using lavatories, baths or washing equipment previously used by men. Clearly, this makes a good excuse for anything untoward which may befall an innocent maiden, and is slightly more credible than the traditional kissing a frog.

If (some) women live in fear of lurking sperm, how much more are they concerned about the possibility of giving birth to animals?

It was current along the Atlantic seaboard of America in the mid-1930s that a girl had hatched an octopus egg – presumably nurtured in her womb, presumably taken on board whilst bathing. And a nurse 'died in terrible agony' when a snake which she was nurturing in her stomach bit her. In this case, it appears, she had been put on a diet and the snake, annoyed by the shortage of food, had decided to eat its host. (Snake-eggs, some believe, may be ingested by drinking from a garden hose. There's sympathetic magic for you.)

Snakes, again no doubt because of their shape, have oft been accused of springing from the ground and penetrating ladies – the fear becomes a mythical reality. It is interesting to note that the 'subtil serpent' of Genesis, which is now represented as curling round the apple-tree chatting matily to Eve, originally went up inside her.

Said Rabbi Jose: 'Why is it that many kinds of magic and divination are only found in women?' R. Isaac replied: 'Thus I have learnt, that when the serpent had intercourse with Eve he injected defilement into her, but not into her husband.' R. Jose then went up to R. Isaac and kissed him [Et tu, Jose?], saying: 'many a time have I asked this question, but not until now have I received a real answer.' (83)

This information appears in other sources, but it was too much for the editors of our present Bible, who arranged the transformation in about 500 B.C.

It's one thing to nurture someone else's egg in your bosom; another to be fertilized by an animal. Mrs Joshua Tofts of Guildford was frightened by a rabbit, and gave birth to a litter of rabbits (26), she said. That was in 1727. Later, she admitted the deception.

Since then, the public has been regaled with tales of animal births from time to time, and almost every old-established community, it seems, has a whispered account of such an occurrence.

Whenever the husband is away for a long time – at 'the wars' for example – there is always the danger of his spouse giving birth to animals. Often, it is an officer's wife, and she gives birth to a litter of alsatian pups. The combination of officer's wife and alsatian seems inevitable; there is, one feels, a level below which the story would fail to satisfy. Terence Rattigan catches the mood nicely (72). Why the mismatched chromosomes choose to represent the father wholly is unclear.

Presumably such women are worried by telegony, a concept – possibly even now – as widespread as it is false. The belief is that impregnation by a particular sire can affect all future offspring, and the famous example is Lord Morton's Foal. Lord Morton produced a hybrid from a quagga stallion and a chestnut mare. (This was at the beginning of the nineteenth century, before the quagga became extinct.) Subsequently the mare produced three foals (in three pregnancies) by a black Arabian stallion; all the foals showed 'distinct quagga-like stripes, "proving conclusively" that the germ cells of the mare had been "infected" by the quagga' for all time (30). It has not been possible to replicate this result (using a zebra instead of a quagga), neither is there any evidence either from years of well-documented breeding of all sorts, or from physiological knowledge.

Even so, it used to be thought that for a woman to produce children by the dead husband's brother (if she had already children by her dead husband) was uneugenic (30). Presumably it would not be entirely unexpected if the products of the two unions bore some similarity. Why it should be 'uneugenic', with or without telegony, escapes me.

The production of large numbers of children is something which catches the public fancy, though 10 seems to be the absolute upper limit since reliable records began (40). However, before science was quite as scientific as we now believe it to be, strange events were reported from time to time such as that reported on a plaque in an abbey near The Hague. In translation, it reads:

> Margaret, daughter of the illustrious Lord Florent Count of Holland, and of Mathilde, daughter of Henri, Duke of Brabant, Sister of William, King of Germany, being 42 years of age, was delivered on the Friday before Easter, at 9 o'clock in the morning, in the year 1276, of 365 babies male and female which (in the presence of several great lords and gentlemen) were arranged in front of the font and were all baptized by a bishop, the males being christened the same name, namely Jean, and the females Elizabeth. All died soon after, as did the mother, and all were buried in the same sepulchre (74).

Probably what we call a 'hydatidiform mole' (bunch of grapes pregnancy), which is what happens when the chorionic villi get out of control. Doubtless the bishop and the members of the court were somewhat myopic, a condition exacerbated by the mother's being the king's niece.

*　　*　　*

The apparent opportunities for medical students to have fun in and out of the dissecting room are obvious. A widely-told story concerns a student who borrowed a set of male genitals and went out for some fun. After an evening's drinking, he concealed himself in a doorway with his trophy, and practised flashing, only to be interrupted by a young policeman: 'What's going on here, then?' The student dropped the parts and took to his heels. The policeman shone his torch on the ground, and went out like a light.

A variant for less hardy company concerns a student who borrowed a finger before setting out on a train journey. He arranged for the door of his compartment to be improperly shut, so that a porter on the platform gave it a hefty shove as the train drew past him. At that signal, the student threw the finger out of the window, uttering a suitable yell of pain. The porter is said to have fainted – presumably his cause-and-effect reasoning wasn't working too well.

If that story is an ambiguous WTS funny story, the next surely bears the classic WTS stamp – since telling it tends to give rise to a particular sort of silence. In fact, it's a 'head-dropper', a name I bestow on a piece of information, such as 'my mother's dog has died', which leaves one cold, therefore speechless, and looking at the ground. So this WTS is a head-dropper.

Some medical students acquired a leg from the dissecting rooms and put it in a girl's bed; they then concealed themselves to enjoy the fun. The girl returned to her room, undressed and got into bed. There was no sound. Uneasily they conferred – what should they do? They decided that the best thing would be to creep slowly away, which they did. The following day, they had no need to go to the trouble of making discreet inquiries – the news was soon abroad that the girl had been found rigidly clutching the leg, staring, staring in front of her. She has not spoken since.

In most museums of pathology, there are various creatures displayed in jars. It may have been at that same medical school where some students connected electrical wires to a preserved cyclops baby so that it could be made to wink at passers-by.

Tim overheard someone, who knows a girl, whose boyfriend's sister is a nurse at Addenbrooke's Hospital (how's that for a foaf's pedigree?), explaining that this nurse had told of some foreign medical students who went into the mortuary and propped up a corpse, giving it a cup of coffee to hold. When the porter went to collect the body, he fainted, and was last seen being carted out on a stretcher.

A story which is gaining ground as I write is of a woman who went to the doctor with a pain in her face. The doctor examined her, and asked her to remove her dentures. Under the upper plate was lodged a tomato pip, which had germinated, and the roots were 'several inches' into the gum – and growing round into the brain, presumably. If they're not now, they will be in a telling or two.

A friend was accosted by an elderly porter at a country station whilst she was waiting for a train – a very difficult situation from which to escape. He explained to her in great detail the horrors of eating tomatoes, for the pips germinate inside you and give you cancer.

Gooseberry pips – and, I'm told, apple pips – collect in your appendix and give you appendicitis.

My grandfather used to scrape the loose scales off his sardines – a tedious ritual – since his pet theory was that the scales 'formed a lining on the inside of the stomach'.

Some people don't like flowers on the table, 'lest the pollen

78

should get into their food,' said I, 'and they give birth to a buttercup,' added my father.

Sydney Garfield (35) said that he was told the following story by a dentist who wished to remain anonymous; he calls him Dr Firenzi. Firenzi was asked by a patient, Steve Pulaski:

'Dr Firenzi, could you extract a tooth for my mother? She has a terrible toothache.'

'Of course,' Dr Firenzi replied, 'Bring her to my office whenever you like.'

'That's impossible, Dr Firenzi, my mother is paralysed and can't move.'

Steve offered to pick up Dr Firenzi Saturday noon . . .

Steve took Dr Firenzi to their walk-up tenament apartment. Steve's mother was stout, about fifty-six years old, sitting immobile in an overstuffed chair, head rigidly fixed, staring wide blank eyed . . . Dr Firenzi soon saw the long neglect demanded, that not only the seemingly single pain-causing tooth be removed, but all . . .

Carefully, Steve holding the flashlight, Dr Firenzi cleaned the area, applied anaesthetics and medications, and extracted the tooth. Healing was satisfactory. Every Saturday, guarding against infection, Dr Firenzi cautiously removed another tooth. On his third visit Dr Firenzi was amazed when Mrs Pulaski, with her eyes and a slight nod, directed attention to the fact that she could move the fingers of her left hand. With these fingers she gestured towards her extracted teeth. Regularly every week, Dr Firenzi told me, it seemed as if by magic, as each additional tooth was removed, Mrs Pulaski would demonstrate another moving part of her body . . .

Paralysed Mrs Pulaski started mobilizing, tooth by removed tooth – finger by hand – by right foot, by right molar – by left leg. She got better and better . . . She was born again . . .

This case is exceptional . . .

A man, reportedly a homosexual, was taken to the casuality ward of a hospital with a small pineapple juice bottle inextricably inserted. The doctor, whom the teller averred was his father, could not think how to pull it out without breaking it, but at last inspiration came. He inserted a straightened and corkscrewed coat hanger in the bottle, filled it with plaster of paris, let it set, and was then able to pull out the bottle. As he did so, the young, naïve student nurse at his side said: 'However did he swallow it in the first place?'

It may have been at the same hospital where a young man of like persuasion minced painfully into the casualty department and confided that he 'seemed to have sat on something.' On examination, the 'something' turned out to be a length of stiff, thick-walled rubber tubing, which was stuck fast. An operation was needed to remove it, and, do you know, they were actually *selling tickets* for the operating theatre? A local anaesthetic was used and it was the patient himself who enjoyed the proceedings most of all!

Talking of back passages, it was during my national service attachment to a military hospital that I first heard about a patient in the officers' wing, a national service second lieutenant who was as unpleasant as some national service second lieutenants could be. What's more, he was much less seriously ill than many of the other patients, and managed to upset them considerably. One day, a walking patient from the other officers' ward put on a white coat and approached the dozing offender. He grabbed the patient's chart from the end of the bed and affected to study it. Then he turned to the patient.

'Good morning,' he said, in a curt tone which brooked no nonsense. 'Turn on your face and pull down your trousers. I'd like to take your rectal temperature.'

The patient had no second thoughts – they had clearly understood the seriousness of his condition at last, and sent this visiting specialist. He turned on his face, and pulled down his pyjama trousers. The visiting specialist inserted a greased daffodil in the appropriate orifice and slipped away – much to everyone's delight.

4

The Famous Whale

How are you? How are you? I r'member your face, but I can't
put a name to it.

— Hippy Damer to Queen Victoria

I have long held a theory, borne out by the telecoverage of
jubilee walkabouts, that the Royal Family must think that
'the people' are a happy lot. The reason is that the aura
surrounding royals is such that it makes people smile, stretch
forth their arms to touch (shades of the King's Evil), and
utter banalities which become pearls of wisdom.

There are, of course, those who grudge the Royal Family
everything they have, and they it is, no doubt, who tell us
with satisfaction that such and such member of it is mentally
under-privileged, if not actually suffering from Down's syndrome (which presumably does not exhibit its usual mani-
festations on royal visages).

Radio reporters at jubilees should be restrained from
asking citizens: 'Where have you come from to day?' This
was one of the two questions that kept hitting micro-
phones with a dull clunk last week. The other was: 'What
did the Queen/Prince Philip say to you?' The answer to
this, as often as not, was: 'Where have you come from
today?' — Paul Ferris.

Currently, a foaf who knows an under-footman at Buckingham Palace tells of the secret forays which the Queen
makes late at night, emerging from a side door of Buckingham Palace and window-shopping in Piccadilly, Bond
Street, Oxford Street and that area.

The Sultan of Turkey has a ready and kindly wit,
which has served him well on occasion. Once, when he
was walking through the outskirts of Constantinople, he

noticed some men at work on the road. It was a hot afternoon, and he remarked to the nearest: 'Warm work, eh?'

The workman laughingly assented.

The purpose of including this wenge little story is to set
the record straight. It was published in the early 1970s, as an
example of the ready and kindly wit of a certain king. (...
'Hot work,' quipped his affable majesty. The workman
laughingly assented.)

Serendipitously, I found the version quoted above in one
of the volumes (62) which I keep for following Lord
Chesterfield's advice. So don't be taken in by the tale when it
turns up again.

When the lowly meet the great what is said is of little importance – it's the fact that it's said at all. The following may be the origin of a WTS, or it may itself be one.

Franklin D. Roosevelt never backed away from a good practical joke and, in fact, thought up quite a few himself. Once he read that people at social functions pay no attention whatever to the murmured words that are required under given circumstances. A famous hostess, for example, bidding her guests good-bye after a party, had said to each of them, with a smile on her face, 'It was a terrible thing for you to have come. I do hope you never come again.' And the departing guests, each busy framing his own proper retort, had not even noticed what she was saying. Mr Roosevelt decided to test the thing. He chose a big White House party, where the reception line was half a mile long. As each guest came up and took his hand, the President flashed his celebrated smile and murmured: 'I murdered my grandmother this morning.' According to the popular story, not a single guest was conscious of what he said. One former associate of Mr Roosevelt, however, denies it. He said a certain Wall Street banker was in that reception line, arrived in front of the President and heard the words: 'I murdered my grandmother this morning.' The Wall Street man then said: 'She certainly had it coming,' and passed on (82).

If more evidence of the aura of the great be needed, I can recall a study wherein people were asked to estimate the heights of the famous, and everyone accredited them with more stature than they possessed. Thus it is that their feats of observation, memory and endurance are reputedly greater than those of ordinary mortals.

That great men manage with far less sleep than the rest of us is often heard.

Some supermen don't wait to have it claimed for them, but advance the claim themselves. John Wesley said that he found five hours completely restful. Napoleon boasted that four were enough for him, and Edison professed to get on with even less.

But the common man would do well to save his admiration for other aspects of these heroes' careers. They were all colossal egoists who affected singularity, and whose word, in this one respect, is open to question. Wesley's greatness did not lie in the field of scientific observation; he was a firm believer in ghosts, poltergeists and witches. Napoleon so wore himself out bragging every morning how little he had slept the night before that he usually dozed off in the afternoon. Indeed, in this particular, it is a matter of satisfaction to remember that he fell asleep during a most critical period of the Battle of Waterloo, while Wellington, who professed no superhuman powers of sleeplessness, remained wide awake. And Harvey Firestone, who knew Edison as well as any man then living, said that he had a good laugh every time he heard how little Edison slept. To be sure, the Wizard of Menlo Park allowed himself only a comparatively short period for sleep at night, but he took cat naps throughout the day which brought his total to the average. (31)

Anyone who is 'great' may be invested with this aura of insomnia – you name them, they're sleepless. The number of reports received about the sleeplessness of its key men may be a measure of the state of a nation.

A sleeping Edison tale:

One night, the inventor and his assistants laboured until 3 a.m. Then the work was interrupted while a breakfast of ham and eggs was served. As the food was being brought in, Mr Edison fell asleep at the table. The others quickly removed his plate of ham and eggs from in front of him and substituted a plate with a few crumbs and scraps of food on it. In a few moments, Mr Edison awoke. He glanced down at the empty plate, patted his stomach with satisfaction, burped lightly, and said 'Well, let's go, boys!' (82)

I wonder who was kidding whom?

One of the most ludicrous of the many indications of superhuman powers of the leader that are advanced by sycophantic admirers is that he can 'wear out' a dozen secretaries and whole cadres of assistants. In the telling, it is implied that the Great One pits himself against a horde of subordinates and vanquishes them – thinks more thoughts than they can comprehend, dictates more than they can transcribe, and exudes more energy than they can cope with.

This, of course, is sheer nonsense. The really great men of the world have produced their thoughts without one millionth of the clatter with which empty men conceal their total lack of thought. Plato, St Paul, Shakespeare, Newton and Einstein together, in their whole lives, probably didn't use half as much secretarial assistance as a fourth vice-president needs on an off-day. Anyone of a fussy and self-important nature who has power over others and can compel them to suit their time to his whims can wear them out, but his doing so is a mark of greatness only in his own estimation. (31)

C. Northcote Parkinson has suggested that an office-staff of 1,000 people is of sufficient size to occupy itself full time with sending and receiving inter-departmental memos. In my own experience, the obfuscating output of a man who dictates woolly rubbish to his secretary (who can't spell or write English either) is responsible for much of the time wasted in this great country of ours. I have seen more than one body of enormous self-importance, who has explained how he cannot possibly live without a secretary and then, when he at last achieves the status-symbol, proceed to bore the poor girl to tears. Other secretaries, of course, claim to run the office, or the great man. Those who do, don't tell you about it.

In the days when the bellows of church organs were pumped by hand there was a story of a muscular rustic who boasted that he had pumped a tune which a visiting musician had been unable to play. (30)

What about the powers of observation of the great?

Superman can read 'at sight', can 'grasp the meaning', of an entire page, or even of an entire book, by 'photographing' it with a glance. The standard version of the myth is often assigned to Theodore Roosevelt; a friend brings him a book, and asks him his opinion of it. The President accepts the book and seems to be fingering it idly while they chat for a few minutes. The friend, on taking his leave, says that he will be interested to know Mr Roosevelt's estimate of the book when he has read it. 'I have read it,' says Mr Roosevelt (who by the way, has been retarded as a reader when a child because of poor eyesight) 'while we were talking.' And sure enough, to his visitor's amazement, he shows a detailed knowledge of the book!

The possession of this talent has been applied to almost every distinguished figure in the modern world except Helen Keller ... (30)

When superman is not reading a book by flicking through the pages, he saves time by 'expert skipping,' whatever that is. 'How,' we are asked, 'does the expert skipper know what to skip without reading it first ... One must not mistake expert skipping for skipping by an expert ...' If one has some knowledge of a subject it is possible to assess a book on that subject by looking at the index, and then reading on select topics. This can be done in a few moments. And surely we all have a selection of pet words which we use to test dictionaries?

In the case of Roosevelt above, the aura of the great ensures that he gives the impression of detailed knowledge. I wouldn't have let him get away with it myself.

Great men also have wonderful memories – or so it is said. Certainly a man's name is a precious thing, not to be trifled with, and if you are expected to know it, great will be the shame and the humiliation of you don't. So it is that the troops often believe that their commander knows every one of them by name: this is just one of the ways in which he gains their respect. Of course, if like the general he says cheerily: 'Good morning, good morning!' it is quite reasonable for Harry and Jack to believe that he actually knows them. And nobody is going to step forward, salute smartly and ask: 'What's my name, Sir?'

Here is a story which demonstrates the phenomenal memory of Disraeli. Dizzy quoted Gladstone in the House, whereupon the Grand Old Man jumped up angrily, shouting: 'I never said that in my life!' Disraeli stood stock still for three minutes; then spoke the whole of Gladstone's speech which contained the offending phrase. (34)

From the higher echelon of the services, public and military, to those of academe. Every centre has its tramps and drunks, and there is often a story attached to certain individuals that they 'were once university professors' (though this may happen only in university towns, and be believed and promulgated only by those who would derive pleasure from seeing the holders of chairs in reduced and pathetic circumstances.

After the Hungarian uprising of 1956 ,when large numbers of refugees arrived in this country, I heard of a factory which took many of them on to its payroll. The story was soon abroad that so and so had been a cabinet minister, another a professor and so on. Since none of them could speak English, there was no way of checking. That is probably why none of them was an artist or a musician.

Some years ago, there approached Cambridge from the North a couple who became known as The Parcels People. They had piles and piles of parcels, which seemed ever to grow. They spent the day moving the collection along the verge, and the night under polythene sheeting which protected the parcels and themselves. The route they would take, who they were, and why they were thus behaving was the subject of wide speculation, but was never revealed. There were tales of a large car (Bentley or Rolls-Royce) arriving in the dead of night and its occupants providing The Parcels People with nourishment. At last, they had a fire in their parcels, which turned out to be largely old newspapers, and disappeared.

But they were not forgotten. A recent account (4) suggests that The Parcels People were none other than Rita Bandaranaike Obeyesekera and her adopted son.

The story was told that they went into a fish and chip café near Stamford and proffered a cheque in payment, which the owner refused to accept. The Parcels People then told the café owner to ring a certain number in London, which he did, and the voice at the other end of the line told the owner that the cheque would be honoured as the people concerned were very wealthy.

Unfortunately, we are not told whether or not he accepted the advice.

It was in the thirteenth century that the news of the Wandering Jew, who had taunted Jesus on the way to the crucifixion and had been told by him to 'go on forever till I return', first reached Europe. In 1228 an Armenian Archbishop, who was visiting St Albans in England, reported that this character, Joseph Cartaphilus by name, lived and was widely renowned in the Orient; and in 1252 this statement was confirmed by other Armenian pilgrims to the same monastery. This information was promptly recognised and hailed as a most weighty proof of Christianity, and continental writers did not fail to apply its full apologetic force against Jews and heretics. Stories of his odd experience multiplied. In most of the accounts the Wandering Jew had forsaken his false faith and adopted the true faith of Jesus, in contrast to the obduracy of his fellow Jews; several versions however have him remain a Jew, refusing to acknowledge through baptism the truth to which his own unique career testified, and thus typifying the attitude of all Jews. (88)

Perhaps the Parcels People were the Wandering Jew in modern dress.

When it was decided to tidy up the basement of the old Zoology Department at Cambridge, there were found to be heaps of old bones belonging to nothing in particular. The local rag-and-bone man was summoned, and given ten shillings to load his cart. As his horse clip-clopped down Pembroke Street, he was arrested by a wild shout: 'Hey, stop!' A dishevelled figure, waving his umbrella, stepped out into the roadway and climbed on to the cart, examining the bones, making little grunts of satisfaction. 'I'll give you a guinea for these, my man,' said the Professor of Zoology, 'if you'll just turn round and take them up the road for me.'

Many stories with a similar ring are told of the collection of scrap metal for the war effort. Railings were cut down and dumped – it was supposed to make people feel good, but when their contributions were left to rust in the area, their attitude turned somewhat sour. Queen Mary did rather well. She would tour the Norfolk lanes with a vehicle, pointing her umbrella imperiously at ploughs, harrows, tractors and so on. Apparently the technique was to collect them without question, and then to go round later and redistribute them (68).

A foaf is a physical chemist, and he sent a learned paper to a learned journal: in due time it was accepted and he received the proofs for correction. His argument depended on the angle of optical rotation α, and all through his paper, wherever α should have appeared, there was a tiny speck. Puzzled, he took a magnifying glass, and looked at the speck; it turned out to be α. Suddenly he twigged – the last line of the paper was missing; the printer had taken it as an instruction. What was the last line? 'It will be seen, therefore, that α should be made as small as possible.'

A foaf who is a mathematician attended an international conference at Geneva (where else?). One of the 'papers' was

given by a very young, bespectacled man who stepped confidently forward and wrote a single-line proof of a theorem, with which students of the theory of numbers had been grappling for years, on the board. The rest of the time allocated for his paper was taken up with a standing ovation.

Sometimes extreme erudition seems to be unnecessary for securing reward. A man in the U.S.A., I read in some unfortunately mislaid source, was awarded a Master's degree for sitting in a cupboard for three days. And another foaf was awarded a first class honours degree in philosophy for answering one of the questions: 'Is this a fair question?' That was all.

Have you noticed, by the way, how people always get *first class* honours degrees? You either read an 'ordinary' course or you read an 'honours' course. Honours is graded 1, 2.1, 2.2, 3. As people always get first class honours, so are the sons of proud parents 'managers' of something. And academic suicides (or any young academic who dies) are always 'brilliant'.

In Cambridge, our stories are usually of 'Oxford dons in the quad;' in Oxford, perhaps, they are of 'Cambridge dons in the court.'

So, an Oxford don greeted an old student in the quad: 'Ah, Wilkinson . . . was it you or your brother who was killed in the war?'

This was doubtless the same Oxford don who stopped to discuss some weighty matter in the quad and then, when the discussion was over asked: 'Now, which way was I going when we met?'

But we should consider awarding the palm to two Russian Grandmasters who sat opposite one another at the chessboard for thirteen hours, until at last one of them exclaimed: 'My God! Is it my move?'

A number of special tales attach themselves to the wives of professors. One, for example, was famed both for her wealth, and for the exquisite meanness of her dinner-parties, at which there would be a carefully calculated allowance of one sausage per guest. And her standard line as she served each guest the solitary delicacy was: '*Dooh* let me know if you haven't got a sausage – some of my friends tell me I cheat.'

Other lines ascribed to professors' wives are: 'What a pretty tie ... it just matches your eyes.' On entering a house lovingly restored by the architect husband of the recipient: 'It's amazing what you can do with these poky little houses.' And, the conversation having turned to cephalopods in general and octopuses in particular: 'I can't imagine what it would be like to be embraced by a beast with eight testicles.'

Dr John Campbell (1708–75) looking into a pamphlet at a bookseller's shop liked it so well as to purchase it; it was not until he had read half through that he discovered it to be of his own composition (85).

And so to the arts. Was it the pianist Arthur Rubinstein who was asked how long he practised each day? And did he reply: 'I don't practise at all. If I don't know the music now, I never will.'?

Perhaps. But we all know that recording techniques are now at such a stage of development that a work can be produced without flaw by careful editing. Is it a vile calumny on the name of a world-famous musician that he is so temperamental, and such a perfectionist, that his recordings are carefully pieced together by engineers, bar by bar? Anyone who has seen and heard him will know that this is absolute rubbish. I will not name him; if I do, I will certainly be told sooner or later that what I say is true.

James McNeill Whistler was asked by a wealthy woman to authenticate a painting: he has to do so in a court of law, goes into the witness box and answers one question. Afterwards:

Lady: How much do I owe you?

JMcNW: One thousand dollars.

Lady: Why, you don't mean to charge a thousand dollars for a minute's work?

JMcNW: Not at all, I charge a thousand dollars for the labours of a lifetime (34).

This story bears a remarkable resemblance to an incident in the celebrated Ruskin v. Whistler libel case. Discussing a nocturne, counsel observed that '200 guineas was a stiffish price.' and questioned Whistler on how long it took him. Eventually, they agreed that it took perhaps two days, one for the main painting, and the second for finishing off.

Counsel: Do you mean to say that you ask 200 guineas for the labour of two days???

Whistler: No, I ask it for the labour of a lifetime.

Since this is in the court records, it is more likely to be the true version.

Both bear a similarity to the story of a plumber who submitted a bill for half a guinea for changing a tap washer. When asked how he made up this exorbitant charge he replied: 'Parts and labour, sixpence; knowing how, ten bob.'

There is a story (85) of an enthusiastic admirer of Tennyson, who accompanied him on an afternoon stroll round and round the terrace at Aldworth. She remained silent, lest she should stifle some priceless utterance. At last the Great Man said: 'Coals are very dear' and his companion, having no ready answer, was silent still. On the next circuit, he said: 'I get all my meat from London'. There's no answer to that either. Third time round he stopped by some drooping carnations. She waited with bated breath – some immortal comment on the passing of the beauty of the blooms? 'It's these cursed rabbits!' he said. That was their afternoon's conversation.

The point about great men is that they ought to be able to touch us because they have mundane thoughts, and eat, drink, sleep, etc., like everyone else. And yet they are expected to be perpetually intense; no doubt some of them are, but that spoils it for the others. I remember an hilarious evening spent looking at Siegfried Sassoon's irreverent collages in art annuals. Please don't forbid great men a sense of humour nor expect continual intenseness.

To deny an expert human feelings is as great a mistake as to expect him to be able to pronounce authoritatively on any field, allied or not to his own. There is no telegony of knowledge. The great writer is not necessarily a great speaker, and vice versa, as many commissioners of work have found to their cost. The less we know of a compartment of knowledge, the more hazy its boundaries. We don't expect a doctor of medicine to be able to treat the guinea-pig, but (if we are not scientists) we may understand no difference between a geneticist and an atomic physicist.

On the other hand, there's always the possibility that the Great Man would *like* to talk about something other than his own speciality. Stephen Potter, an expert on S. T. Coleridge, made the point: 'The man who depended on mugging up the subjects of his weekend fellow guest never went very far.' And he continued:

> On one occasion, for instance, hearing that Dr Lowes, the expert on Coleridge, was to be present during a weekend holiday, [Protheroe] spent the previous month (he was a very slow reader) trying to memorize the facts of a small, mass-produced life of S. T. Coleridge printed in the These Men Have Made Their Mark series.
>
> By the Sunday evening, when the visit was coming to an end, he realized only too well that as yet *no reference to Coleridge had been made*. During a pause in the conversation, he decided to speak.
>
> Protheroe: I am right in saying, I believe, that there are two versions of the 'Ancient Mariner', and they are not the same.
> Lowes: 1798 and 1800?
> Protheroe: 1798 and 1800 . . .
> Lowes: Yes – they are not the same.
> Protheroe: Not the same.
> And here the conversation ended. (70)

Perhaps we can all sympathize with Protheroe. Unless I know my company, I am loathe to bore them with small-talk. I once sat through the President's tea-party at Queens'. unable to think of anything which I thought anyone would think worth saying. At last, I asked him some question about a long-case clock in the Gallery. He didn't know the answer, and that was that.

Although the good Lord Chesterfield (1643–1773) may have refrained from naming the gentleman in the following story on the grounds of delicacy, I somehow doubt it. In a letter to his son, he wrote:

> I knew a gentleman who was so good a manager of his

time that he would not even lose that small portion of it which the calls of nature obliged him to pass in the necessary-house; but gradually went through all the Latin poets in those moments. He bought, for example, a common edition of Horace, of which he tore off gradually a couple of pages, carried them with him to that necessary place, read them first and then sent them down as a sacrifice to Cloacina; this was so much time fairly gained, and I recommend you to follow his example ... Books of science and of a grave sort must be read with continuity; but there are very many, and even very useful ones, which may be read with advantage by snatches and unconnectedly: such are all the good Latin poets, except Virgil in his *Aeneid*, and such are most of the modern poets, in which you will find many pieces worth reading that will not take above seven or eight minutes. (85)

The great and famous (two characteristics which are by no means synonymous, especially since the explosion of the media) are well known to be tremendously mean. A man of my acquaintance was approached on a London station by a very rich man indeed who suggested that they share a taxi 'to save money'. Well, why not? In this conversation, someone will sooner or later say that it's only by behaving like this that the rich become rich. And then someone will bring in Paul Getty's coin boxes, and Gulbenkian's using a London taxi 'which will turn on a sixpence, whatever that is'.

And everyone knows of the television celebrity who looks so cheerful on the screen, with his dispensations of largesse, the ideal man to open the local fete. But the village couldn't afford the £500 fee he demanded for the privilege ...

One of the ways of becoming the subject of a WTS is to be either specially good or bad. The good become better; the bad become worse.

I will leave questions such as whether or not Christianity was really invented by St Paul, and merely point out that the leader of any movement tends to fulfil prophesies, and accrete legends of his fitness of purpose, in much the same way as Nostradamus and Mother Shipton – of whom more later – have been credited with feats not theirs. Moreover, the movement will accrete unto itself elements of the mores of the people it serves, to gain acceptance. However, I'm not discussing this.

Instead, let us look at the Russian monk Grigori Yefimovitch Rasputin. Born in 1871, he lived quietly in his native village until 1904, when he became notorious for his extravagant teachings – almost Messianic, save that he advocated sin in order to obtain repentance and salvation. Obviously likely to attract a following: if people are going to sin, they might as well have the guilt taken out of it.

He was presented at the Russian court in 1907, and when he improved the health of the Tsarevitch Alexis, the doctors having given up hope, it seemed a miracle, at least to the Tsar and Tsarina. After that, he was unable to do wrong and in spite, or because, of this was hated by the bulk of the nation and most of the nobility.

How he finally met his end is the subject of some conjecture, but it is generally 'known' that he had some secret power of immortality, and that he had to be killed many times before he would die.

The deed was carried out by Prince Youssoupov, supported by his cronies. Youssoupov prepared his properties in the basement of his palace, and persuaded Rasputin to visit him in the strictest secrecy. It is here that the accounts become difficult to disentangle.

In one (53), Rasputin is offered wine (liberally dosed with poison), but asks for tea. This is provided, and Rasputin then eats three pieces of chocolate cake, each containing enough hydrocyanic acid to kill an army. 'It's very sweet,' he says. Youssoupov then pours him a glass of poisoned wine – he drinks it; then another. Rasputin says: 'There's a bitter taste in my mouth, give me some more wine to drink, I feel thirsty.' He drinks two more glasses of the poisoned wine. Youssoupov is, as you can imagine, on tenterhooks. He goes upstairs and tells his waiting cronies what has – or hasn't happened. He takes a revolver ,and goes down again. Rasputin complains of a heavy head and a burning in the stomach. He drinks another glass of poisoned wine. Youssoupov shoots him 'through the heart', Dr Lasovert comes down and pronounces him dead.

Somehow, the enormity of what they have done to the monarch's favourite sinks in, and their only thought is to get

"ODD! THIS CAKE HAS A BULLET IN IT"

rid of the body. They discuss this, and then Youssoupov shakes Rasputin – the latter opens his eyes, stands up, foaming at the mouth, and crawls up the steps from the basement, making his way to the outside world. Purishkevitch shoots him four times and stamps on his face. Youssoupov belabours Rasputin with a rubber truncheon until he (Youssoupov) becomes limp and loses consciousness.

Every time one sees (or hears) a reconstruction of the murder, it appears that something new has been added to the sequence of events – to make Rasputin seem that much more evil. So he is bashed with candlesticks, thrown out of windows, and still comes back for more – it's like Tom and Jerry.

What actually happened, as I said, will never be known with certainty, but there is some extra material which casts doubt on the story above. Another account (94) says that Rasputin ate biscuits, not cake; Maria Rasputin – his daughter – says that her father never ate cake. No poison was found in the body.

A third account (59) speaks of 'cakes' rather than 'pieces

of cake' but points out that Rasputin *never* ate cake. However, having waved the plate away, he changed his mind, and ate two. Here, Maria is reported as saying: 'I'm positive that my father did not eat the poisoned cakes, for he had a horror of sweet things.' As for the wine, she said: 'Doubtless the poison had not dissolved.' Careless.

However, she goes on to put her finger on the spot:

I am convinced that certain details given by the assassins were added partly to make the story more picturesque and partly to excuse the slaughter; for since it was a question of doing away with a being whose devilish vitality resisted cyanide, it would be understandable that the five conspirators, in their terror, should riddle him with bullets.

In this account, by the way, Youssoupov does not become senseless through his exertions with the truncheon, but goes to speak to the policeman who comes to see what is going on. Nevertheless, 'going back to the dead body after the policeman had left he found that Rasputin had changed his position.'

Well, there we are. I'm in danger of concluding merely what we all know – that historical research is very difficult, and you have to state what you believe to be the most likely to be true, based on the evidence available to you at the time. To reiterate my thesis: the good get better, and the bad get worse. Whoever heard of St Francis kicking a dog?

Remember when the Duke of Wellington was accosted by a man in the street with the words: 'Mr Jones, I believe?'

Said the Duke: 'If you believe that, you will believe anything.'

5

The Whale at War

And ye shall hear of wars and rumours of wars: see that
ye be not troubled

Matthew 24:6

It is particularly apposite to start this chapter with a Biblical
quotation, as one of the earliest WTSs is to be found in the
Bible; (Judges 12:5,6):

> And the Gileadites took the passages of Jordan before
> the Ephraimites: and it was so, that when those Ephraim-
> ites which were escaped said, Let me go over; that the
> men of Gilead said unto him, Art thou an Ephraimite? If
> he said, Nay; Then said they unto him, Say now Shibbo-
> leth: for he could not frame to pronounce it right. Then
> they took him and slew him at the passages of Jordan: and
> there fell at that time of the Ephraimites forty and two
> thousand.

The fear of the enemy infiltrating one's country is obviously
a real and powerful one. In Holland, there is a seaside resort
near The Hague called Scheveningen, and the legend has it
that this name, being difficult to pronounce, was used during
the Second World War as a Dutch Shibboleth.

> Suspicious native (pointing to sign 'Scheveningen'):
> Read that!
> Enemy infiltrator: Skreveningen
> BANG!

The problem with Scheveningen is not so much one of getting people to say it as the fact that it is not particularly
difficult to say: with a few seconds tutelage, I was able to
pass muster as a Dutchman – on that one word. There are
sounds in Dutch which are much more difficult for the alien
to pronounce, and far less avoidable than Scheveningen; 'Ik

ga' (I go) for example. If you can fool the natives with your everyday speech, specialities such as Scheveningen are child's play.

(I would like to be able to report that the Dutch Bible gives the clue which links Shibboleth and Scheveningen, but it doesn't.)

In Denmark, spies were asked to say something like 'rødgrød med fløde', a redcurrant pudding with cream.

In the war which I remember, we had our own ways of identifying spies. My grandfather was turned down by the War Office when he offered to resume his First World War commission (and after all, he was seventy in 1939). He became quite neurotic about spies, and spent much time identifying them and their meeting places and bombarding officialdom with letters. If the country was full of old soldiers doing that, it's a wonder that the machinery didn't become quite clogged. However, Gpa told me that if I suspected someone of being a spy, I was to accost him and ask him to say: 'Where were the wise women?' No doubt the spy would have done the honourable thing on finding that he'd been rumbled by a six-year-old, and have allowed me to lead him to the nearest policeman.

Spies, of course, had to come down by parachute, and it was reported (89) that they 'wore spring heels and bounced even when they jumped down from lorries.' More realistic, of course, was the belief that they were equipped with bicycles so that they could move swiftly about the country.

My vivid imagination has always boggled at the thought of how one would arrange for oneself and bicycle to land safely on the same parachute.

Be that as it may, it appears that those who avoided giving an impression of the old umbrella-mender and were able to pedal away from their landing-places, were further weeded out by riding on the wrong side of the road.

The few that were left were confused by the lack of direction-signs, and would inevitably have to stop and ask the way. The standard answer to this was 'Turn left, left, and left again.' The spy would ride off, and his informant would raise a posse to await his return.

As everyone knows, spies or escapers on the continent wore rough serge clothes and berets and masqueraded as dim relatives of members of the underground. In Britain, on the other hand, spies tended to be disguised as nuns.

A foaf was sitting opposite a nun on a train; she was reading the Bible, but dropped off to sleep and the book fell on the floor. She bent down to retrieve it and her habit slid up to reveal a hairy arm with a portrait of Hitler tattooed on it.

One wonders whether this story had any connection with the Father Brown story (19) wherein Brown recognizes Flambeau, the arch criminal:

> I suspected you when we first met. It's that little bulge up the sleeve where you people have the spiked bracelet.

Unfortunately, once a dangerous type is identified, it may have far-reaching effects on the innocent.

Perhaps now it is hard to credit this nation of animal-lovers with ill-treating dachshunds just because the breed had a German name, but the state of hatred ran so high that this did happen. Even the disclosure that Dachshund (German) = Brocker (Anglo-Saxon) = Badger-hound (English) failed to stop the rot.

However, even if the Brocker couldn't be disguised, his owner obviously could, and yet there were reports of men with close-cropped heads and wearing monocles stirring up racial hatred at public meetings. Since it is incredible that a genuine enemy infiltrator would be so stupid as to continue to exhibit his stereotyping characteristics, one may perhaps assume that such stories were an oblique way of scornfully pointing out unthinking Germanic military stupidity.

So it was that there was a much-told spy rumour, wherein a tradesman called at a newly-let house to solicit custom (that dates it!) When the door was opened, he recoiled in horror, for there was the brutal Prussian who had commanded the prisoner-of-war camp in which the caller had spent the First World War.

Before France was occupied, there was a story current (8) that the station-master at such and such a station had been discovered to be a spy. The way in which it happened was as follows. The authorities noticed that somehow the Germans always managed to bomb the station when there was a troop train there, and sometimes, it seemed, the station-master would even delay the train until the enemy bombers arrived.

An intelligence watch was therefore kept on the man, and one day, when there was a troop-train standing at the platform, the stationmaster's young son ran up to him and told him that he was wanted on the telephone. 'Impossible!' said the stationmaster, 'The line has been cut.' 'No,' urged the boy. 'It's the telephone in the cellar.' The intelligence man went to investigate, and heard a German voice on the other end of the secret telephone in the cellar. The spy was unmasked.

A number of WTSs concerned with the war would appear to have had their bases in psychological wishes that there would be no war (the Beaverbrook syndrome), or that the war would be over by a certain date. This is hardly surprising. Underlying rational man is a seething mass of irrationality, compulsion mania, sympathetic magic and the rest. Why else should there be scarcely a paper without a horoscope?

I am sure that I was not alone in saying: the First War began in 1914 and lasted until 1918; the Second War began in 1939 and will therefore stop in 1943. That didn't work, but it was a comfort. Later, I said: 1914 to 1939 is 25 years, therefore the next war will start in 1964. Happily, that didn't work either. It is a complex game of 'she loves me, she loves me not'; we know the answer we want, and we keep picking flowers until we have a simple majority. If that doesn't work, we say 'things go by opposites'. In spite of the palpable futility of the exercise, we may continue with it *ad nauseam*.

Marie Bonaparte, a psycho-analyst, gives a full account of several widespread myths, and examines the psycho-analytical rationale underlying them (8).

She reports her first in twenty-nine guises; it runs as follows: A foaf is driving along when he sees a woman by the roadside seeking a lift. He stops, and the woman turns out to be a fortune-teller, who says that before he gets home there will be a corpse in his car. She then follows this extra-ordinary piece of news (which he doesn't believe for one moment) with the prophesy that there will be no war (if the story is told before the war) or that the war will end on a certain date (if the story is told during the war). Other versions fortell Hitler's death, he being the force behind the war. But to return to the corpse. The fortune-teller is set down, and the traveller continues on his journey: however, either he takes on another passenger, or he calls at the house of a friend who seeks a lift for himself (or another), or he comes across a road accident and takes the victim to hospital. Whatever the detail, he takes a passenger, and the passenger dies in transit. The story, it appears, was current not only in Europe, but also England and America.

There was another type of story which connected a pre-diction with Hitler's death and the end of the war – 'the myth of the guessed money'. In this story, the fortune-teller by some concatenation of circumstances is able to say how much someone else in the story has on his or her person. When surprise is expressed at this correct disclosure, the for-tune-teller then goes on to say: 'It's as true as that Hitler will be dead on such and such a date, and the war will end.'

The corroboration of a known fact by a prediction seems an odd way of gaining credence. But this has happened with such well-known seers as Nostradamus and Mother Shipton, on to whose original works have been grafted, from time to time, updatings which make the putative originator seem that much more reliable. And the more right they seem to have been, the more likely to be right they must be in their predictions. A tortuous argument.

But the principle is ambiguous: we think also that *because* the fortune-teller was right about the money – and there's no proof that she was – then she *must be* right about the awaited event.

Marie Bonaparte sees in the myths of war which she quotes 'traces of ancient human sacrifice, of sacrificial gifts and of continence observed as propitiation.'

She then goes on to say:

in our succeeding myths, the terror aroused in nations by the threat of enemy aggression gives rise to another mechanism, more primitive and even more simple, by which to control anxiety: the plain denial of the enemy's menace.

Whether or not this needs any deep, primitive psychology I find it hard to say. It is firmly rooted in people that they forget the unpleasant and remember the pleasant (such as those long, hot summers of childhood), or that they don't hear what you are saying if they don't choose to (selective auditory response), or that they stuff unopened bills behind the clock on the mantelpiece and wait for them to go away (Dun's syndrome).

A story prevalent in France just before the 1939–45 War (8) concerned an English motorist touring on the continent in his Rolls-Royce. He comes up behind (or rounds a corner to find) a German panzer division. He cannot stop in time (or his brakes fail) – he closes his eyes and waits for the crash. There is a crash but when he opens his eyes, he finds that his car is more or less undamaged, and the tank is in pieces – it is made of plywood. On the continent, the reciprocal story circulated: a German was touring in England in his Mercedes, and the same thing happened.

Apparently this is a common trick amongst great powers. When Harold Macmillan visited Moscow in the 1960s, one of his aides somehow became detached from the touring party, and found himself able to take a closer look at the ultra-modern fighters parked around the airfield. They turned out to be made of plywood.

Much of the equipment which drives through Red Square on May Day is made of plywood. And no doubt 'they' say the same thing about our demonstrations of might.

However, if 'there's a war on', and you can't imagine the enemy out of existence – nor, instantly, beat 'em – then you can try joining 'em. Stories of this genre, the friendly enemy, may give some comfort to the fighting forces, but are not calculated to please those making their sacrifices on the home front. As far as I can gather, they are widely believed, and a television advertisement for a well-known brand of cigar has done nothing to dispel them.

One gets the impression that 'the trenches' were some sort of maze where one might turn a corner to find oneself face to face with one's adversary. Thus they exchanged gifts at Christmas, or instantly agreed to part, each refusing to harm the other. Indeed, in some versions, they are politely told that they must have taken a wrong turning, and directed back to their own lines by the 'enemy'.

They play football in no-man's-land, they draw water from the same well, they exchange warnings of impending attacks. And if further proof of the friendly enemy be needed, there is always the one about the troops firing only when observed by their superior officers. Nobody really wants to fight a war on somebody else's behalf, so there were always pacifist wiseacres suggesting that the leaders of both sides should be put 'in the ring' so that only they would suffer. Not that one disagrees with the sentiment, but it shows no regard for the complexity of the reasons for waging war. What it does show is the belief, real or wished for, that all 'ordinary people' on both sides are peace-loving beings, and all brothers under the skin.

The seige of Ladysmith during the Boer War was conducted in an unusually gentlemanly way (86).

There was no shooting and no fighting on the Sabbath, and often the Boers took a holiday from shooting after any particularly busy day. Firing rarely began before breakfast or continued after tea, and there were regular half-hour intervals for meals.

At Christmas,

some plum puddings were even provided by the Boers, who sent over shells marked 'With the Compliments of the Season', which contained puddings partly cooked by the heat of the explosion in the gun barrels.

Every war produces its crop of people who are lucky to be alive, saved from the enemy missile by a pocket Bible, or a locket containing a picture of mother, over the heart. There are certain conventions: it has to be a Bible or a picture of mother: *Alice in Wonder-Land*, or a picture of a racing

pigeon are excluded. And it goes without saying that the protective article has to be over the heart because in spite of all we know to the contrary, people are always shot through the heart.

Although some of the reality can now be told, it is from the historical point of view of some importance to preserve the inaccuracies that went with it. The term 'Hitler's Secret Weapon' was applied equally to a particularly nauseating carrot jam and to the much more fearsome 'death ray'. The realities of wireless and the fantasies of science fiction made it easy for people to believe that our enemies were about to perfect a death ray, and no doubt our enemies believed the same about us.

There was certainly an updated story that 'we' had a secret ray which could stop the engines of cars or aircraft, and the proof of this lay in an incident which would occur, usually on a road on the South or East coast, to a foaf. He would be driving along when, all of a sudden, his engine would cut out. He would get out of the car and start to investigate the fault, when along would come the local policeman.

'Just wait a moment, sir, and it'll cure itself,' he would say, and it would. It was the defensive ray, out of hand again.

No one familiar with the secret war of Dr R. V. Jones (49) can have failed to have been amazed at the incredibly Teutonic fact that the Germans always managed to pick a code-name for their secret weapons which had some obscure mythological connection with the weapon itself. Be that as it may, if you have some device, such as radar, which enables you to locate your enemy consistently better than you would be able to by chance, it must eventually dawn on him that you have such a device.

And this was the problem with radar. It is said that the rumour was deliberately spread that our pilots were fed quantities of carrots to improve their night-vision – and this was why they were so successful. Although carrots do contain the makings of vitamin A, which itself is essential for the production of visual purple (the pigment in the retina which enables vision in poor light), there should be enough vitamin A in the normal diet, as many foods other than carrots contain it.

Since much innocent laughter was generated by accounts of guns with curved barrels for firing round corners, it is probably well to set the record straight by quoting an authority (48).

> The curved-barrel Maschinenpistolen were a remarkable wartime development which, however, well illustrates the gusto with which the German High Command entered into futile projects which promised relatively little and diverted valuable production time from more conventional weapons of war.
>
> The base for the Krummlauf device was an MP44 to which was fitted a curved-barrel unit with suitable mirror sights attached to the muzzle. It has been said, though never satisfactorily proved, that the idea was to provide a means for firing around corners without exposing the operator to hostile fire; and another version tells of the necessity for dislodging hostile Russians from tanks.
>
> A third story, however, tells that the curved-barrel was an unexpected by-product from a project originally intended to provide a device by which firing trials could satisfactorily be accomplished without recourse to the conventional ranges; it is said that from this it was thought that other, more useful purposes could be served – and it may also be that the last tale is the most likely of the three.

However, to increase the life of the barrels, it was necessary to pierce them with holes to slow the bullet down. This in turn drastically reduced the efficiency of the gun, but they rationalized this by saying that it was 'envisaged solely as an ultra-short-range weapon.'

On the home front, there was plenty going on, though much of it seemed to have little to do with any war which was, or was not, being fought (89). One of the most widespread upheavals after the departure or redeployment of the menfolk was the evacuation of thousands of children from dangerous centres to various parts of the country.

Soon there was a rich crop of 'evacuee stories'. The

press offered prizes for them and the public responded by foisting off all the traditional tales about urban urchins in the country. One of the most-quoted was that of the couple who found their two billeted children lying at the extreme edges of the bed, with an empty space between. When asked why, they said, 'Well, where are youse yins going to sleep?' In another version, the children were found lying under the bed – 'this is where we always sleep at home'.

Several evacuee stories from this source (as indeed, are several incidents from this source) are woven into a current highly recommendable musical (50). There is also a story from Sir John Hammerton (41).

Two East End lads billeted in a noble mansion were waiting impatiently for their breakfast. At the top of the table sat the elderly *châtelaine* and behind her stood the butler. When it looked as if they were going to be late for school, one of the lads said to the butler: 'When's that bloody breakfast coming?' The old lady said: 'I'm so glad you have said that. I have been wanting to say it for years.'

There were other opportunities for bravery on the home front. A foaf was firewatching during the war, when a stick of incendiary bombs came down on the town hall. He raised the alarm, and then suddenly remembered that the mayor's regalia was inside the town hall. So he dashed into the smoke and flames and found a huge and heavy chest, which he started to drag out. It was such a strain, and the smoke was so choking that several times he nearly gave up, but his civic pride spurred him on. He got the chest out, and collapsed on the steps. He woke up in hospital to find himself a hero. The chest had been full of hand-grenades and ammunition for the Home Guard. He was awarded the George Medal.

There is a military analogue of this story in *A Bridge Too Far*, where a soldier gives up his life to rescue a parachute pod of what is thought to be vital supplies, but which turns out to be – berets.

The other side of the coin showed the looting firemen. All over the country, every night, Woolworth's 3d & 6d stores were being bombed, and those who ought to have been protecting the property were in fact making off with huge quantities of ladies' underwear and stockings and selling them on the black market. (Compare the New York power failure of July 1977.)

To call into question the phenomenal accuracy of bomb-aimers is near heresy, though there is no reason to suppose that 'we' were any more accurate than 'they' until advanced methods became available.

There was, however, plenty of reason to suppose that 'they' could bomb accurately because of the current stories. And with tortuous reasoning, if 'they' were accurate, then 'we' must be as well, except that experience showed that 'they' weren't.

'Evidence' came from *The Times*, the clergy, and the air-raid wardens. There was a letter to *The Times* from a First World War pilot (89):

Persons should on no account look up at the sky when enemy aircraft were overhead, he said. The white blobs of numerous upturned faces can be seen from an aeroplane at a considerable height and form a good and tempting target. Those unable to contain their curiosity were advised to shade their faces with their hats.

A clergyman addressed the Chester and Warrington Methodist Synod:

German airmen are careful not to bomb breweries and maltings in Britain because Hitler knows that if Britons go on drinking at the present rate, we shall lose the war.

As for that well-known street-cry: 'Put out that * * * * * * * light!':

It was a flattering tribute to the navigational powers of the Luftwaffe to suppose that it could pick out, from the heart of a darkened island, a message in code flashed from a solitary light bulb, torch or cigarette in an anonymous suburb.

ARP Wardens were necessarily unpopular at times, and the butt of an obvious WTS:

A gossip writer reported that somebody had met somebody else who said that near Aldgate Pump lived a man, normally unemployed, who had been heard to boast that he had got an ARP job, that his wife and family were evacuated, and that he had never been so well off in his life, the more so as he lived rent-free – 'nobody pays rent round here, there's a war on'.

Back to the front.

Two soldiers are overtaken on the road by a peasant who offers them a place in his cart. When they get in, they find a young nun already there. Further on, with nothing but open country around, she professes to be at her destination and asks to get down. Before saying goodbye, she tells the soldiers to be unafraid, that the war will end before summer, that they will suffer no hurt and that all will be well.

She then disappears and the soldiers see a piece of paper on the ground, dropped, they think, by the nun. They pick it up and deeply moved, recognize the very image of their fellow-traveller in the holy picture of St Theresa of Lisieux (8).

Positive identification of the Angel of Mons?

Reports of weeping effigies and pictures of female saints, not to mention the BVM, were not uncommon. Presumably it is not manly to cry, but what else can a statue do? Well, it can move, particularly if it is an assemblage of pieces. Thus we find stories of people being 'frightened to death' by the heavy hand of a suit of armour falling on their shoulders (how is this known to be the cause of death, any more than that the whole of his life passes before the eyes of a drownee?), and Salvador Dalí (23) tells us the following:

> The story has often been told of the Andalusian anarchist who during the Civil War walked up the steps of a gutted and profaned church with the grace of a torrero, drew himself up to his full height before a crucifix whose Christ wore long natural hair, and after having insulted Him with the most atrocious blasphemies, spat into His face while with one hand he brutally seized the long hair which he was about to tear out. At this moment the Christ's hand became detached from the cross and His arm, which was articulated, fell on the shoulder of the Andalusian soldier, who dropped dead on the spot. What a believer!

It was certainly well-known that 'they put bromide in the tea/coffee' to reduce randiness, though such measures were hardly necessary in view of the strenuous régime we had to follow at the time. Such stories seem to have been prevalent everywhere and through the ages – 'the myth of the doctored wine' (8). It is reported that the sexual prowess of recruits always diminished, and who can be surprised at that? In France, the wine was doctored; in Poland it was the coffee. In South Africa, it was the food itself which contained a mysterious anaphrodisiac called 'blue-stone' – as it had allegedly been in the First World War. In Germany, iodine was put into the coffee, and soda into the meat.

The story doesn't stop there:

> even more widespread is the belief that saltpetre is an anti-aphrodisiac [sic] and is secretly introduced into the food at colleges, prisons, and other places where amorous impulses are thought to have ungovernable force. It is safe to say that there is not a boys' school or an army camp in the country in which this myth is not entrenched. (30)

As the enemy was conquered, the Royal Engineers were

the first into towns and cities, in order to get the services working again. Many is the German town where a couple of sappers stayed on after the war to become the Mayor and the Chief of Police.

Many readers may have forgotten (or never heard of) Manning Coles, creator of British Agent Tommy Hambledon. It may be to Manning Coles that we owe the story of the sappers who stayed on, or Manning Coles may have been inspired by the story.

The appropriate potted plot (20) is as follows:

An amnesiac is fished out of the sea in January 1918 and taken to a German Naval Hospital. He is christened Klaus Lehmann, (he can't remember who he really is) and starts life in Germany. In 1923 he meets Hitler, after the latter's release from prison, and through this meeting takes up a post with the National Socialist Party. Ten years later he is a deputy of the Reichstag, when the shock of the Reichstag fire suddenly brings back his memory – he is none other than Tommy Hambledon, British Intelligence Agent. As he comes to terms with his knowledge, he is offered the post of Deputy Chief of Police, which he accepts. He makes contact with London via a radio play, *The Radio Operator*, which contains coded messages in its morse background. In time, of course, he becomes Chief of Police, but his double role becomes more and more dangerous until he is forced to change clothes with a corpse with whom he can be confused. Tommy Hambledon returns to England, laughing as he hears on the wireless of the 'cowardly and brutal murder of our Chief of Police, Herr Klaus Lehmann ... faithful servant and leader of the Reich and a trusted and beloved friend of the Führer himself, who will pronounce the oration at the State funeral on Tuesday next ...'

In Switzerland, the following story cropped up time and again (8). Germans had orders to create 'incidents' in Switzerland, and cross one of the Rhine bridges and assemble in the village square. Suddenly a bugle sounds, the Germans are surrounded by Swiss soldiers and taken prisoner without a murmur. Because nothing seems to be happening, another contingent of Germans strips naked and swims across the Rhine, with their equipment in rubber bags. They are also rounded up, the bags are impounded, and they are made to parade in the nude.

Both sides of the channel had stories of pellets which would turn water into petrol. A convoy would find itself low on petrol in some deserted spot with the inevitable solitary farmhouse occupied by an old couple. They would ask for water, and fill up their tanks with it. Then they would drop in the secret pellets, and, lo! The water was turned to petrol. This again seems to be a modern version of the philosopher's stone, the elixir of life, multum in parvo, a three-course meal in a pill.

It is a pity that the secret has been lost – it would have saved all those expensive operations in the North Sea.

Unless, of course, the whole North Sea Oil boom is a myth invented by the government, aided and abetted by the media, to disguise the existence of the petrol pellets.

Our Ministry of Information, it seems, started the rumour that we were able to set the sea on fire (using petrol pellets??) in order the prevent invasion of our island. If the effect of this technique gave comfort at home, the effect it had on the enemy was devastating.

There were many stories of how many times the Germans had attempted to invade, and how many of them had been burnt in the blazing sea – up to 350,000 at one attempt. From there it was but a short step to tell how the Germans were committing suicide in droves, or having to be forced on board landing-craft at gun-point, so frightened were they of being fried in the sea.

As for those who *had* been fried in the sea, the British collected the corpses, identified them in some macabre sorting office, loaded them into planes, and dropped each on his home town.

SPLAT! SPLAT! SPLAT!

Sometimes the M. of I. machinations backfired. For example, they are supposed to have disseminated a story that the Germans had invented a bomb 'which would kill 100,000 people and take 10,000 prisoners.' They were soon receiving desperate requests that the rumour should be denied. Apparently, it had been thought that it was so silly, that nobody could have believed it. I cannot fathom why they would have started such a rumour in the first place.

Eventually the European war came to an end, and within three months that in the Far East was terminated by one of the most significant events of our time – the dropping of the atomic bomb: nothing has ever been the same since. It is not surprising that the bomb gave rise to its own WTSs, among them one which I remember hearing very soon after the event – that all that immense energy was contained in something the size of a matchbox. It is interesting that the same idea was current in Japan (46).

The bomb is the size of a matchbox. The heat of it was

six thousand times that of the sun. It exploded in the air. There is some radium in it. I don't know just how it works, but when the radium is put together, it explodes.

So the war was over, but not everyone knew this. Every so often, a Japanese who hasn't heard the news appears: some rejoin a society which they must find unbearably alien, others disappear into the jungle again, refusing to believe the news. Who can blame them? There can't be many left now.

On the other hand, there were several wanted war criminals not accounted for, and only the elapsing of their maximum life-span will assure their seekers (or their seekers' successors) that they are gone for ever.

Wanted men for obvious reasons acquire an aura of mystery. Just as we excuse fox-hunting by drawing attention to its inefficiency (probably in the same breath as saying that it is more humane and efficient than shooting or gassing), so do we feel some sympathy with the one who gets away. (It depends upon what he's done, of course.) The human emotions are complex and fickle. Ronald Biggs robs an incomprehensible sum of money from a public body, on public transport, escapes from a penal institution, and because of the ethos surrounding that particular case (everyone having forgotten Driver Mills) becomes a folk hero of sorts – until, that is, he takes the British Navy for a ride, an action which is just not on.

There is something romantic about a war criminal living a hard and simple life in the South American jungle – we forget why he's wanted, and even feel that he's paid for his sins many times over by his banishment.

And it may of course be something about the mysterious South America – where Col. Percy Fawcett disappeared, where there are strange, misunderstood artefacts of great antiquity, where there is gold to turn a man's head, and whence, some say, Jesus escaped a couple of millennia ago to start a secret sect.

One of the latest stories to emerge from the South American jungle is of a vast community living in luxury below the surface, heated and lit by an everlasting power source of great antiquity. The community speaks German, because some 3,000 German troops escaped there in 1941. We avidly await further news, but it would seem that the original informants have mysteriously disappeared.

6

The Technological Whale

> The Church welcomes technological progress and receives it with love, for it is an indubitable fact that technological progress comes from God and, therefore, can and must lead to Him.
>
> Pope Pius XII

Technology, and matters technological, have given rise to many WTSs, some of which have appeared in other chapters. A sub-set of technological stories – those pertaining to the motor-car – is grouped in the next chapter.

However, a few general technological WTSs of the sort you might hear whilst grasping a glass in one hand and a sausage on a stick in the other will not be out of place here.

A young couple (foafs, of course) purchased a house which they decided to modernize and decorate. They were following the instructions from a weekly partwork for knocking front and back rooms into one. They spent one Sunday morning breaking through the wall; then, tired and dusty they set out to the local for a lunchtime drink. When they returned, they could not believe their eyes: the house had fallen down. The instalment about putting in an RSJ to support the load didn't come out until the following week.

A friend was working in an old factory where there was some massive, old-fashioned machinery which they wanted to get rid of. First, they advertised it, but no one wished to know. Then they started to take it to pieces, but the job was so slow that they calculated it would take about three months – and then there was the problem of getting rid of the parts. So eventually they swallowed their pride and sent for some machinery demolition experts. On the appointed day came a little man with a little hammer and a big man with a big hammer. In complete silence, and with a look of intense concentration on his face, the little man tapped the framework in various places; then chalked a cross at a certain spot. The big man swung his sledgehammer and, lo! the frame fractured. They carried on thus and, by lunchtime, the machinery was a heap of scrap on the floor ready for carting away.

A foaf had a vacation job working in a power station. When switching in an alternator, it has to be run up to speed and synchronized. This is done by watching three lamps flashing (he said) and comparing them with the three of the new alternator. The foaf somehow ran his alternator back to front; one set of lamps was flashing red, blue, yellow, and the other red, yellow, blue. Undeterred, he waited until both the red lamps were on, and threw the switch. There was the most tremendous explosion, and the alternator sailed out through the roof of the power station. Luckily no one was hurt.

Things usually sail out through the roof. A foaf was working in a gunpowder factory, where they use heavy flywheels to crush the ingredients. If something goes wrong with the mixture, the flywheel sails out through the roof.

A friend of mine who is interested in the restoration of old buildings heard of a factory chimney which had to be removed because it was unsafe. Fantastic – all those lovely bricks. He went to negotiate a bid and was overjoyed to find that he could demolish the chimney in return for the materials contained in it. The deal was clinched and he went to look at the chimney. And he found that bricks used for building chimneys are, not unnaturally on reflection, tapered to allow for the curvature.

However, he was luckier than the foaf who set up as a demolition contractor, and also, as it happens, undertook to remove a chimney. He had a brilliant idea: he sealed the base, filled it with water to a depth of a few feet, and put in an explosive charge. When he set off the charge, the force was distributed equally in all directions, a ring of bricks was shot out, and the chimney settled, slightly shorter than it had been before.

The same story is told of an IRA attempt to blow up an electricity pylon: a charge was placed on each of the four legs, and set off. The effect was to shorten the pylon without interrupting the electricity supply.

A building worker was on the ground in charge of that end of a rope and pulley mechanism for transporting building materials up and down. He was holding the rope and at the top was a barrel, which a mate loaded with rubble. On the occasion of which I am speaking, it seems that the barrel was loaded such that it was heavier than the man on the ground and he, not having the presence of mind to let go of the rope and step out of the way, was pulled up into the air. On reaching the top, he struck his head on the pulley, and at the same time the impact of the barrel on the ground caused it to split so that its contents fell out. The balance was now such that the stunned worker fell to the ground, dragging the barrel up to the top again. When he reached the ground, he let go of the rope, and down came the barrel striking him a final blow.

The late Gerard Hoffnung told this story at the Oxford Union (47) but I first read it in bold type on the front page of a newspaper some years before. I remember this particularly, as I was acting as a guinea-pig for some lip-reading classes at the time, and told the story with illustrations on the blackboard.

It purported to come from Aahrus, which is suspicious, for, as I have said, in Denmark Aahrus jokes are as Irish jokes in England. At one time, the Hoffnung record was so well-known that no one would have dared to tell the story as true, but it will doubtless be back any silly season now.

Just as the famous Orson Welles broadcast spread panic in America before the Second World War, so, it appears, were a huge number of people taken in by the *Alternative 3* programme shown on ITV in June 1977 (it was originally scheduled for 1st April). Personally, I found it hard to believe that anyone could have been fooled by the hammy interviews with pseudo-scientists, but it will serve to reinforce the story that human artefacts were found on the moon by both Americans and Russians – and that both are keeping quiet about it. Could the story have started in the film *The First Man on the Moon*, where Kenneth More landed, only to find an empty baked beans tin?

The reciprocal of the artefacts-on-the-moon story is the belief that the whole of the moon landing programme was simulated in the television studios. This is quite widespread – especially in Mexico, where they laugh at you if you suggest that it really happened. The purpose of the elaborate fabrication is not stated.

No book of WTSs would be complete without some reference to 'parascience'. An excellent feature in *New Scientist* (64) sums up the 'evidence' for the Bermuda Triangle, Flying Saucers and Spoonbending, not to mention the Miracle of Fatima. But these are isolated subjects in parascience, which covers a vast range of unexplained happenings and artefacts. Its literature grows as rapidly as that of any of the more conventional sciences. Disproving such a widely-reported phenomenon as flying saucers is difficult; proving it, if the evidence should become available, would be much easier. Stonehenge as an eclipse-predictor (43) is either a colossal coincidence, or an example of how proper analysis can enable a topic to pass from parascience to science (though discovery of its possible mathematical purpose by no means answers all the questions about Stonehenge).

It is commonly felt that conventional religion has let us down in not providing the answers to the basic questions mankind dares to ask it. Religious faith, it seems, is not enough; parascientific faith comes much more easily, to some. According to John Morley, 'The next great task of science is to create a religion for mankind'.

What *was* Pope Pius XII trying to tell us in his Christmas message of 1953, quoted at the head of this chapter? Technology may lead us to God, but will that God turn out to be the one envisaged by the Pope . . . ?

I have explored in a different place (78) the relationship between religion and science; between the 'mysteries of the ancients' and modern technology. To my mind, this is what parascience ought to be trying to achieve – and can achieve, if properly applied. When (I'm that confident) it provides the answers, let us hope that they will be recognized and welcomed.

7

The Whale at the Wheel

The modern motor-car is in all cases a comfortable con-
veyance, and in the more expensive types it embodies a
greater degree of luxury than any other medium of
locomotion, except perhaps the Atlantic liner.

Edward Cressy

Has any single invention had such a profound effect on mankind as the motor-car? Apart from its superficial value for
getting things from A to B, it has its role as a symbol for sex,
status and Lord knows what-all. I look forward to the role of
the motor-car in shaping twentieth-century man and his
society coming into perspective; we will no doubt learn
something exceedingly profound about ourselves when it
does.

As befits its stature, the motor-car and the way of life it
has engendered have provided several widespread WTSs,
many of which have already enjoyed a rich and varied life.

A foaf saw a motor-car advertised in the local press for £5.
Of course, he couldn't believe his eyes – this year's model?
All those extras? Well, if it was true, he was on to a good
thing; somebody had to be there first and it could be he. So
he rushed round to the address, and there was this woman,
and she showed him the car, and the registration documents
and so on, and it all seemed to be in order. Without asking
too many questions, he gave her the fiver, and she gave him a
receipt, and he drove it away. Later, he found out the truth –
the woman's husband had left her, and asked her to sell his
car and send him the proceeds.

In another version of the £5 car, the truth is made only
too plain before the purchase. 'The car's down in the
garage,' the woman says. 'But there's one thing I must tell

you before you look at it – my poor (choke) dear husband (choke) committed suicide in it . . .'

And it needs cleaning out somewhat.

An emancipated Edwardian motoring WTS. The Vicar of D—— was cycling along one evening, when he came across a stranded motorist whose acetylene lamps had run out of water. Having ascertained the nature of the problem, 'That's easy,' he said, 'we can use the water with which the Good Lord provided us.' Making sure that the coast was clear, he stood on tiptoes on the running-board, and peed into the container. 'That's all I've got,' he said. 'You'd better do the other side.' The motorist removed her goggles. 'I'm awfully sorry,' she said, 'the Good Lord forgot to make the proper provision.' A member of the suffragette set.

A foaf had a vintage Austin – mechanically immaculate,

but bodywork tatty. Well, he was driving along – outskirts of Nottingham actually – when he was stopped by the police. They had a good look at his car: tyres OK, steering good, lights working, nothing falling off – couldn't find anything wrong. 'Right,' they said. 'We want to test your speedometer and brakes. Drive along at a steady thirty and we'll follow you. Then when we blow the horn, you do an emergency stop.' So the foaf did as he was bid, and hearing an almighty blast on the horn stepped on the anchors. There was a most tremendous crash as the police car ran into the back of his Austin. It was, of course, another vehicle which had blown its horn.

A young foaf went for a driving test with his motorcycle. 'Drive round the block,' said the tester. 'And when you see me step out into the road, do your emergency stop.' So the motorcyclist rode round the block, but on returning to the appointed place was surprised to a see a crowd gathering in that normally quiet street. By the roadside was a mixture of bodies and motorcycle. The tester had stepped out in front of the wrong rider.

The normal practice in this country when one is selling a car with a noisy gearbox (so I'm told) is to fill it with saw-dust. But a friend of mine tells me that he has heard, once from a Chilean and once from a Venezuelan, that the South American custom is to fill the gearbox with mince. There's opulence for you.

In the days of my youth, a group of us used to hunt the quiet lanes of East Anglia in my 1923 Rover 8. We would often hear of elusive cars which had been bought new before the war (i.e., pre-1914) and kept immaculately by their proud owners. At the beginning of the war (i.e., 1939) they had been laid up – raised on blocks, covered in grease and dust sheets. But the old man (if it was an old woman, she had had a chauffeur) had died, and it was found that he had left instructions in his will that the precious car should be burnt on a ceremonial pyre after his funeral. We never tracked the tale to its source.

A foaf was getting ready to go out one evening, when he

noticed from his bedroom window that there was a car blocking the mouth of the drive. As he had some time to spare, he ignored it, expecting it to go away. However, nearly an hour later he found that it was still there, and as he could see no signs of life, he walked down to investigate. There, inside, was a couple, coupled. 'Thank God you've come,' shouted the man. 'Something's gone in my back, and I can't move.' So the foaf went back and called the police, and they called an ambulance, and the fire brigade. The upshot of it was that the firemen had to cut the top off the car to lift the man out. While they were waiting for the other stretcher, the officer-in-charge said to the woman: 'I'm frightfully sorry that we've had to cut up your husband's car.' She smiled wanly, and replied: 'That's all right. It's not my husband.'

As befits the king of cars, the Rolls-Royce has a number of stories all of its own. Henry Royce used to go down to the works just before knocking-off time on Saturday, cast an eye over a heap of chassis frames and say: 'Well, boys, which one am I going home on today?' And before they left, they built him a car to use that weekend.

The Rolls of legend has a sealed bonnet, which must never be opened except at the factory. And if any driver not trained by the works should take the wheel, the guarantee is instantly void.

Not, of course, that there needs to be a guarantee. There is a well-known Rolls-Royce which was touring in Spain when a half-shaft (sometimes the crankshaft) broke, just outside Madrid. So the family secured accommodation for the night, and sent a telegram to Derby. Almost before daybreak, two immaculately-dressed mechanics flew in with tools and spares, and the family tour was able to continue with hardly a hitch. When asked for the bill, there came the reply: 'No charge, sir. Rolls-Royce half-shafts (crankshafts) *never* break.'

Now I'll tell you the true one, and I do know to whom it happened. His Rolls-Royce broke down on the M1 near Newport Pagnell. He telephoned Derby. 'I should go to a garage, if I were you,' they said. 'Hey, wait a minute,' he remonstrated. 'What about the half-shaft that broke in Spain?' 'Oh yes,' they replied, 'we can send a mechanic if you want, but it'll cost you £100 a day. I should go to a garage if I were you.'

A foaf was going through the customs when he noticed a disturbance – there was this immaculate man, and his be-furred wife, and his Rolls-Royce, and the customs-men were going through it with the proverbial fine toothcomb. And what a fuss the owner was making. And as the foaf watched, he saw the customs officials discover the specially streng-thened springs, and testing the mudguards and body panels, and finding that they were made of nothing less than sheets of gold. The smugglers had been detected.

A foaf was motoring along, when the stream of traffic slowed to a halt, apparently because of some altercation be-tween the driver of a Rolls-Royce and another motorist. One alighted, and twisted off the other's wing-mirror. The other, not to be outdone, did the same to his opponent. As if in slow motion, each perpetrated some unpleasantness on the other: the other retaliated. Never a word was spoken. A crowd gathered in silence. At last, when all the accessories on each car had been smashed, the motorists shook hands, got into their respective vehicles and, amidst the ovation of the crowd, drove away.

The owner of a stately home (not open to the public) is somewhat annoyed to see a car and caravan turn into his drive, park on the verge, and disgorge a full load of family, which proceeds to unpack the well-known folding chairs, tables, gas stoves etc. and prepare a meal. However, he does nothing, but takes the number of the vehicle, and then traces the owner via the police. In the fullness of time, he loads his car with equipment and family, sets off for the suburban semi wherein his unwelcome visitors live, and holds a picnic in their drive.

Lord Montagu of Beaulieu tells a similar story (60) about the owner of a stately home which *was* open to the public. He was

> incensed by the mess and litter left by a party of visitors. He made a note of their address, and the following week he and his family went there and held a noisy and messy picnic on the front lawn of their suburban house.

Later, I heard of a local farmer who was said to have done the same thing.

Talking of trippers, a party of Cambridge people on a gasworks outing to Yarmouth had to help one of their number back to the coach because he was helplessly drunk. On reaching Cambridge, they took him home and put him to bed to sleep it off. When he woke, he was astonished to find himself at home in Cambridge because he hadn't been a member of the coach party but was in the middle of a fortnight's holiday in Yarmouth and had merely fallen in with the crowd of his workmates who happened to be on the works outing. Meanwhile, his wife had reported him missing to the police.

There is a reciprocal version of this tale. A couple went on holiday and thought it would be rather fun to spend a day on an advertised mystery coach trip. So they bought tickets and set off in high hopes, only to find that the mystery destination was their home town. So rather than paying exorbitant rates for the local food, they decided to pop home and cook themselves a meal there. And somehow, they managed to miss the coach back.

A foaf was touring with a caravan on the continent, and ran short of time to catch the ferry back to England, so he had to drive furiously through the night, with his wife having a kip in the caravan they were towing. At length, he had to stop for a pee, and while he was out, his wife woke up and also felt the call of nature. So she left the fastness of the caravan and went into the bushes. And her husband returned and drove off into the night. Luckily (in some ways) the next car along was a police-car, but she still had some difficulty in explaining what had happened.

In a reciprocal version of this story, it is the tired man who is resting in the caravan, and the wife who is driving. For some reason or other, she is forced to stop suddenly, and her husband very unwisely emerges in his underpants to see what the trouble is. As if on a signal, she chooses that moment to drive away.

The moral is: some laws are eminently sensible.

A foaf and his girl-friend were on holiday in a little village in Cornwall. One morning, they planned to drive to the large town nearby to do some shopping; however, they found that the car wouldn't start, so the girl-friend went to the village shop to buy the necessary groceries while the foaf started work on the car. When she returned, she saw legs sticking out from under the car, so she administered a playful squeeze to their confluence, and went into the cottage, where she was astounded to see the foaf enjoying a cup of coffee. He explained that the man under the car was a kindly neighbour, and that he should be coming in any minute now to have his coffee and discuss the car problem with the foaf. The girl-friend explained what had happened, and they sat and waited for the man to come indoors, wondering how to explain the attack. But he didn't come, and he didn't come, so they went out to investigate and found that he was still under the car. They were unable to attract his attention, so they dragged him out, and there he was, nursing a large bruise on his head. 'Something made me bump my head on the sump' he mumbled confusedly. 'Come indoors and have a drink,' they replied, exchanging glances.

Earlier last year, I came across the following:

The Final Curtain

The latest in confidence tricks ... A Surrey couple had their car stolen from their front drive. Four days later it reappeared – with two theatre tickets on the front seat and a note which read: 'Sorry. We had to take your car in an emergency. Please accept the tickets with our apologies.' A few days later they used the tickets and returned to find their home stripped, even to the curtains.

I won't say it's not true, but it has the marks of a WTS. For example, the names, and addresses, not to mention the ages, of the couple are not given. And wouldn't they have reported the loss of the car to the police? So wouldn't the police suspect something? Perhaps not. Perhaps it's true. But I can only say that it has been reported to me as happening to foafs twice since I read it.

One for the road. A foaf was touring on the continent, snaking along one of those mountain roads with a sheer drop on one side. Rather too suddenly, he came upon a sharp bend to the left and not altogether wisely took it on the inside. That day the Gods were smiling, for, coming from the other direction was another car whose driver had been similarly surprised by the bend and had taken it on the outside. So they crossed on a blind corner, each on the wrong side of the road. Somewhat shaken, both stopped, got out, walked back to the bend, shook hands silently, turned, and, without a word, walked back to their cars and drove off.

8

Whales and Other Animals

Animals are such agreeable friends—they ask no
questions, they pass no criticisms

George Eliot

A great deal of energy has been expended on the truth of the
story that Jonah was swallowed by a whale. Those who
think they're in the know say that a whale's throat is too
small to take a man. However, the sperm whale, or cachalot,
does have a throat of sufficient size and it is said that the
skeleton of an 18-foot shark was found in the stomach of one
of these animals. (It is also said that a man in a suit of
armour was found in a shark.)

In February 1891, one James Bartley fell off a whaler and
could not be found. However, the crew at last caught a
whale, and started to prepare it that night. The next day
they attached tackle to the whale's stomach, and hoisted it
on board. Suddenly, the sailors were startled by something in
it which gave spasmodic signs of life. (Shades of *the* WTS.)
Of course – it was none other than James Bartley. However,
he was unconscious, and when he revived had to be restrained as a raving lunatic, but after three weeks of kind and
careful treatment he had entirely recovered from the shock
and resumed his duties. But the whale's gastric juices had
bleached his skin and he never recovered his natural appearance (74).

Frank T. Bullen was more lucky, in a way. He was first
mate of the good whaler *Cachalot*, and was with a crew in a
small boat seeking to entrap one of the parent ship's live
namesakes. The monster smashed the boat, and FTB became
involved with the 'titanic convulsions of the dying cachalot'.
He was much afraid of being swallowed whole, but wasn't.
He was rescued and put to bed for three weeks: 'In my sleep I
would undergo the horrible anticipation of sliding down that

awful, cavernous mouth over again, often waking with a shriek and drenched with sweat.' He returned to work looking ten years older (13).

But what of Jonah? It is the popularizers of the Bible who assumed that a 'great fish' is a whale. And the 'village atheists' have pounced on this and said that the whale has a small throat, therefore it could not have swallowed Jonah, therefore the whole Bible is untrue.

Make no mistake, Jonah was swallowed by a great *dahg* (fish) and not by a *taneem,* the word translated as 'whale' in Ezek 32: 2, or *taneen* Gen 1: 21 and Job 7: 12. (Both these words are elsewhere translated as 'dragon' or 'serpent'.) So Jonah's *dahg* could have been a cachalot.

But to further confuse those who would tell tales of men being swallowed by whales of one sort or another as an oblique affirmation of Old Testament faith, John Miles has suggested that, in any case, the Book of Jonah is a parody (58). For a start, instead of expressing his reluctance to be a prophet in anguished eloquence, Jonah remains silent. And the idea that he actually *pays* for his passage to Tarshish seems as ludicrous to Miles as if Moses had thrown water on the burning bush. And so we are taken from unlikely detail to unlikely detail until the Lord finally comforts Jonah with a gourd, only to send a worm to destroy it the following day, not to mention the wind and the sun.

If the Book of Jonah is a parody – and Miles puts forward a scholarly case for it being so – it is a very amusing one, taken in the context of the minor prophets of the Hebrew Bible.

Writing of the whale (95), Rev. J. G. Wood uses the following words:

> The jaw opens very far back, and in a large Whale is about sixteen feet in length, seven feet wide, and ten or twelve feet in height, affording space, as has been quaintly remarked, for a jolly-boat and her crew to float in.

Ernest Protheroe, FZS, also writing of the whale (71), uses the following words:

> The length of the baleen (16 feet) gives some idea of the size of the Whale's mouth, and it is not without reason that sailors assert that a ship's jolly-boat with a crew complete could row into the cavernous aperture without touching the sides.

I wonder where they got that jolly-boat from?

Whilst wallowing in the luxury of late Victorian natural history writers – fine as long as you can stop when you want to – let us look at Wood, an entertainingly anecdotal writer, on the grey parrot:

> Its power of imitating all kinds of sounds is really astonishing. I have heard a parrot imitate, or rather reproduce, in rapid succession the most dissimilar of sounds, without the least effort and with the most astonishing truthfulness. He could whistle lazily like a street idler, cry prawns and shrimps as well as any costermonger, creak like an ungreased 'sheave' in the pulley that is set in the blocks through which ropes run for sundry nautical purposes, or keep up a quiet and gentle monologue about his own accomplishments with a simplicity of attitude that was most absurd. Even in the imitation of louder noises he was equally expert, and could sound the danger whistle or blow off steam with an astonishing accuracy. Until I came to understand the bird, I used to wonder why some invisible person was always turning an imperceptible capstan in my close vicinity, for the parrot had also learned to

imitate the grinding of the capstan bars and the metallic clink of the catch as it falls rapidly upon the cogs. As for the ordinary accomplishments of parrots, he possessed them in perfection, but in my mind his most perfect performance was the imitation of a dog having his foot run over by a cartwheel. First there came the sudden, half-frightened bark, as the beast found itself in unexpected danger, and then the loud shriek of pain, followed by the series of howls that is popularly termed 'pen and ink'. Lastly the howls grew fainter as the dog was supposed to be limping away, and you really seemed to hear him turn the corner and retreat into the distance. The memory of the bird must have been most tenacious, and its powers of observation far beyond the common order; for he could not have been a witness to such a canine accident more than once.

Another parrot story (77):

> Horse drawn tram services in Douglas, Isle of Man, were disrupted when the horses, which usually stopped only at the conductor's whistle, kept drawing up at a point between two halts. It was found that a parrot lived in a house overlooking the promenade and had got the signal whistle off to a tee.

From parrots to penguins. All the world loves a penguin, owing to the fact that it's bipedal and dresses for dinner. Those of us hedged around with property and possessions turn all shades of green with envy at someone who can swim a few thousand miles, pop out on to an island, and set up house just like that.

The young son of a foaf arrived home from a visit to the Zoo, dumped his duffel-bag, and tucked into a plate of bangers and mash. Whilst trying to elicit from him whether or not he had had a good day, and what he had seen, his mother noticed a movement in the duffel-bag which was lying in the corner of the room. On investigation, the bag was found to contain a baby penguin. The lad denied all knowledge of it – no, he *hadn't* picked it up when nobody was looking. So his mother telephoned the Zoo, and found that it still had the full complement of penguins ...

This bears a remarkable resemblance in essence to an incident which occurred some eighty years before, when a man strolling in Regent's Park came across a large snake curled up in a flower-bed. He called a keeper, who called other keepers, and they stood guard over the sleeping reptile while someone hot-footed it to the Zoo to fetch the snake-keeper. And although the snake was captured and taken to the Zoo, it wasn't one of theirs. This story was reported in the press of the day, and suddenly snake-finding became an epidemic. A London & North-Western railway guard found a twenty-two foot boa-constrictor in his van. And the son of an MP found a huge snake in one of the rooms of his father's London house (34).

The penguin story may have some affinity with the account of the man who was walking along St. John's Wood Road, when he saw a penguin waddling along. The penguin approached him on his stroll. Soon they saw a policeman, and the man inquired what he should do with the penguin. 'Take him to the Zoo, if I were you, Sir,' said the policeman. So the man did. The next day, the policeman was surprised to see the man coming towards him with the penguin still walking by his side. 'I thought I said you should take the penguin to the Zoo,' said the policeman. 'I did,' replied the man, 'and this afternoon, we're going to the pictures.'

Compare this with the shaggy dog story (66) of the barman who – after much preamble – was given a lobster by a grateful customer.

'Thank you very much, sir, I'll take it home for supper.'
'Oh no, don't do that, barman – er, I mean, I'd rather you didn't. You see, he's had his supper. Just put him to bed.'

The father of a friend of mine is an insurance broker – he's in fire, but has a colleague in the motor department who tells the following story.

They received a claim from a motorist the front of whose mini was completely squashed. On the claim form in answer to the question about the cause of the accident, they read 'I was following a circus procession through the town, and it came to a railway bridge. At that moment, a train passed over the bridge, and this startled an elephant which was bringing up the rear of the procession. The elephant sat on the front of my car and that's why it's damaged.'

However, my informant's brother is also in the insurance business, and he avers that the elephant sat on the mini because it mistook it for its circus tub. I remember the story was popular at about the time when the mini came out, and may have some foundation in the unprecedentedly revolutionary design at that time, just asking to be sat upon by elephants.

Sure enough, the elephant story circulated in the world of motor insurance before the time of the mini, and the red mini, which reminded the sedentary pachyderm of its circus tub, was an example of the timeliness of the WTS enjoying a mini-revival.

Elephants seem to be attracted to cars like bees to a honey-pot. Here's one from last summer (39):

I heard a story over the weekend which I find unlikely but I'm assured it's true. A chap took his family to Knowsley Safari Park in South Lancashire. As they were driving around, an elephant got a bit uppity and bashed the car door. They didn't, of course, stop to reason with it, but drove off at high speed to the nearest bar, where the man downed a few swift ones to restore his shattered nerves. On the way home there was a three- or four-car 'shunt' ahead of them. Our man stopped for the vehicles to be got out of the way (nobody was hurt). As he sat there, a policeman came along and asked if he'd been involved in the accident. He replied, quite truthfully, that he hadn't. The policeman looked at the damaged car door and said: 'So how did this happen, then?' All unthinkingly the man replied: 'An elephant kicked it in.' The officer looked very hard at him and said: 'I think you'd better breathe into this bag, sir,' So he did. And he was over the limit.

Three weeks later (39), there was a follow-up:

A week or two ago I repeated the story of the man who had the door of his car kicked in by an elephant in a safari park ... I was assured it was true, but doubted it. Now I get a letter from Robin Mackley which shows how wise my scepticism was. He says, and proves it, that he printed the story in the house journal of John Smith's Tadcaster Brewery as early as November 1976, and it wasn't Knowsley Park, Lancashire, but Flamingo Park, Yorkshire. How nice when one gets the truth at last. But wait ... what have we here? A letter from Patricia Hess of London W8, who proves to me – what is proof? said jesting Pilate – that it happened years ago in New York ...

While all this was going on, I heard the following story from two or three sources.

A foaf drove into a safari park, and his wife ill-advisedly wound down her window for some fresh air – the next thing they knew was that an elephant's trunk was curling through the window in search of sandwiches. Mrs foaf panicked, and wound up the window, catching the elephant's trunk. The entrapped beast, more in dismay than in anger, placed its front feet on the side of the car and pulled. It released its trunk, but dented the car, and the foaf had the problem of explaining the 'cause of accident' to the insurance company.

Two days later, I heard the story again, as follows: A foaf was driving through a safari park when he spotted a fellow-visitor whose car had broken down. He stopped to help, and his wife, sitting in the car, opened the windows because it was stuffy. The wife and the elephant behaved as before, and the incident so shook the foaf that he had a stiff drink before setting off down the M6 for home. Noticing the somewhat damaged car, the motorway police gave chase, stopped it, and sought an explanation. 'An elephant dented it,' explained the foaf, reeking of brandy. To cut short a story of quite sufficient length, he lost his licence.

There is something appealing about the elephant: its looks, its trunk, its smile, its docility *vis-à-vis* its size, the fact that man can bend it to his will – all these give one a feeling of companionship (not to mention a secret superiority). The elephant therefore has a special ethos of, for example, elephant jokes; the production of a set of jokes about anything is an accolade in itself.

But apart from 'why did the elephant paint his toe-nails red?' there are more serious tales concerning the astonishing memory of the elephant. The WTS is of the hunter who somehow wounds a young elephant, which makes its escape. However, it turns up in a circus many years later, spies the hunter in the audience, lifts him out and revengefully tramples him to death. The alternative, not, presumably a WTS, concerns the hunter's performing some service to the elephant – such as releasing it from a snare – and the elephant, spying him in the one-and-ninepennies at the circus, lifts him out and places him gently in the three-and-sixpennies. Those were the seat prices when I heard the tale.

One more tale before I leave elephants.

An old lady rings up the police in a state of great nervousness. 'Officer, there's a huge grey animal in my vegetable garden.'

'Oh yes, madam, and what's it doing?'

'It's trampling all over my cabbages and pulling them up with its tail.'

'With its tail, madam? And what's it doing with them then?'

'If I told you that, officer, you wouldn't believe me!'

I have heard it said that horses are attracted to humans (are they?) because their eyes distort their view of humans so that humans look like horses. However, a moment's thought will show that, in that case, horses would be distorted to look like something else again ... If horses like humans, it's because they know which side out their nosebags are.

A tale of the thoughtful rapport which we would all like to have with the animal kingdom (*cf*. Dr Doolittle), is woven into the message of *Androcles and the Lion* (81). Androcles removes a thorn from the lion's paw, and the lion later rewards him by not eating him when, in his capacity as a Christian, he is thrown to it.

In a shaggy dog/folk-tale version, a mouse gnaws through a lion's bonds, and the grateful lion offers him any reward he cares to name. The mouse asks for the lion's daughter's hand in marriage. The wedding ceremony ends in mourning, when the bride accidentaly steps on her groom.

The following story was told to me by the school-teacher to whom it happened: she was asked by one of her class how to spell 'vulture'. She imparted the necessary information, thinking to herself that at last she was going to see a really creative piece of work. When it was handed in, however, her delight changed its direction, for she read: 'I got a Boots Gift Vulture for Christmas . . .'

Since we're back to birds, I will take the opportunity of recounting a WTS in the making – it occurs in a review of *Inside the Animal World* (15), wherein are found the following words:

> There is also a special chapter on unsolved problems. Myths are debunked, but plenty of mysteries remain, such as; magpies' mass meetings; rooks who light matches and hold the flames under their wings; . . .

This I *had* to explore, so I turned to the book in question. I was disappointed to find that the report was of a crow which liked to sit in the smoke of a straw fire in its aviary, though

> the operation was difficult, because as fast as a match was struck the excited crow would snatch it from one's fingers and hold it under its wing. In its 20 years, the crow fire-bathed hundreds of times.

How I wonder, does one discover that an animal likes taking part in such unusual activities? It is a sobering thought that there may be members of the animal kingdom – perhaps even of the plant kingdom – whom serendipity has not singled out for the discovery of such simple pleasures.

The techniques of book-reviewing are sobering, too.

My father was having some trouble with a blocked lavatory. He took his old-fashioned lavatory brush and broddled it up and down in the pan – then he looked in and – what should he see, but a hedgehog! 'Poor thing,' he thought, 'fancy falling into a lavatory and drowning.' then he looked at his lavatory brush, and found that, owing to the ravages of woodworm, the head had snapped off and was giving an erinaceous impression.

A friend's uncle was a vet, who spent some time abroad in Bagdad. One day, he was walking through the streets when he heard a noise approaching him from behind – on inspection, it turned out to be a pack of rabid dogs coming after him. What should he do? With great presence of mind, he seized a stone from a wall and flung it at the leader of the pack. The leader was hit between the eyes and fell, whereupon the rest of the pack set upon the body, enabling the pursued to make his getaway.

The same tale is told of wolves in Russia; they chase after your sledge in a pack, and the technique is to shoot the leader. Its fellows fall on the body and devour it; this enables you to get ahead before they catch up with you again and you have to shoot another – and so on until you reach your destination.

A similar danger befell Baron Munchausen (63) who was walking in the streets of St Petersburg when he was assailed by a mad dog. The Baron ran towards home, taking off his fur cloak as he went; he cast the cloak down in the path of the dog, which instantly set upon it. Later, the Baron sent his servant for the cloak; it was retrieved and hung in the wardrobe. The next day, the Baron found that the cloak had torn all the clothes in the wardrobe to pieces – how he dealt with it is not told.

It was on the way to St Petersburg on a one-horse sledge that the Baron suddenly spied a voracious wolf gaining on him. To put on speed, the Baron reduced his wind-resistance by lying flat but the wolf continued to gain on them. At last, with a great leap, the wolf sprang, but to the Baron's surprise the animal sailed over the sledge and took hold of the rear end of his horse. This made the horse run even faster, as the wolf ate its way into his body. Always ready to make capital out of his extraordinary adventures, the Baron whipped the wolf into the horse, the shell of the horse fell to the ground, the wolf found himself in the harness, and thus they arrived triumphant at St Petersburg.

While I'm on the subject of the Baron, I will recount one further singular phenomenon, though it has nothing to do with animals. You will have gathered that he was a great traveller and teller of tales, and he recalled an occasion when, travelling through the frozen wastes in his carriage, the postillion put his horn to his lips and attempted to play all manner of tunes – but the air was so cold that no sound came out.

Later that day, they took refuge in an inn for the night, the postilion placed his horn by the fire and, the instrument thawing out, all the tunes he had attempted to play earlier came out, and entertained the assembled company for some time.

Many of the baron's adventures, it should be pointed out, had already befallen earlier explorers.

Fishy stories from Baron Munchausen, a fishy story from Cornwall. While her husband was out in a boat sea-fishing, his wife, who was bathing, found to her consternation that she had lost her wedding-ring. Although she knew it to be fruitless, she searched for some times as one does, before returning to their rented cottage.

In due time, her husband returned home well pleased with his catch and started to prepare it for the table. He was told by his tearful wife of her loss, and was about to wash his hands to comfort her when he felt something inside the fish he was gutting. And do you know what? It was the lost wedding ring!

Ripley tells a wedding-ring story (75):

Mrs A. A. Viel of Greytown, Natal, South Africa baked 150 cakes for the troops in Europe in 1941. She missed her wedding ring, so to save opening all the cakes she sent a note with them. The finder was – of all people – her son, Sgt Ronnie Viel, who by an extraordinary coincidence was handed one of the cakes in London and found his mother's ring in it.

Ripley also reports a watch in a fish, a crab wearing sunglasses, and a goldfish with a hawthorn tree growing out of its head. In another place (74) he writes:

The editor of *The Torch* assures me that the following paragraph which appeared in his newspaper is nothing but the truth.

Seven years ago a farmer in Iowa hung his vest on a

fence in the barnyard. A calf chewed up a pocket in the garment in which was a gold watch. Last week the animal, a staid old milk cow, was butchered for beef, and the time-piece was found in such a position between the lungs of the cow that respiration – the closing in and filling of the lungs – kept the stemwinder wound up, and the watch had lost but four minutes in seven years.

While we're on staid old milk cows, my tail-piece comes from a veterinary research laboratory. There was a man there who had a disembodied cow's udder, set up so that when emulsified grass was fed in, it would produce milk. But the coincidence was that his wife had a supernumary breast . . .

9

The Whale Aghast

You see what will happen if you keep on biting your
nails.

Noel Coward
Message on a post-card of the Venus de Milo

Why, one wonders, should anyone want to tell a story about
some part of the body being snipped, hacked or wrenched
off? And why, once such a story has been told, should the
listener want to retell it as his own? Superficially, our culture
does not admit to our enjoying such tales, so why do they
exist? It sees to me that, placed in context of the broader
spectrum of the WTS, their existence becomes more explic-
able.

One may conjecture that the more ghastly a story is, the
more likely it is to be believed, since the teller is obviously (?)
not telling it for fun. There is a need for the catharsis of
telling others about an accident you have witnessed, or the
death of someone, however remote his connection with you,
and it may be that some people find the same vicarious
pleasure in telling the ghastly WTS. Some are rather like a
particular sort of teenage joke to which those of us with
teenage families are subjected at the appropriate stage of
development, though I do not think that an urge to shock
always lies beneath the telling of a ghastly WTS.

Perhaps I ought to get on with some examples. If you
don't feel strong enough, leave this chapter out. Remember,
however, that having studied it you will be able to laugh in
the face of anyone who tries to serve you one of the golden
oldies.

The first incident happened in a village in North Wales,
which shall be nameless, as there is only one butcher (Jones

the Butcher) there and we don't want to get him a bad name. Jones the Butcher was famed for his sausages, and took a great pride in his spicy recipe, which had been handed down for many generations. Now, accidents happen in the best regulated butcheries, and one day a nest of mice somehow found its way into the mincing machine and – whoosh – there it wasn't before you could say Steele-Bodger's XV. Jones the Butcher looked at the mince, and couldn't see any signs of the unwanted meat, so he shrugged his shoulders and made his batch of sausages – which, as usual, was sold almost as soon as it was ready. The following day, Mrs Morgan came into the shop: 'Would it be possible to have some more of those delicious sausages, Mr Jones? I've never tasted anything quite like them before.'

Before the war, a foaf and his friend were on a walking tour in the Black Forest. Somehow, they lost their way and began to feel rather worried as it began to get dark, for it was a very chilly evening. Luckily, they came across a little cottage, and knocked on the door. It was opened by an old woodcutter: they were given an effusive welcome and ushered into the kitchen where there was a great cauldron steaming over an open fire. They were given large helpings of delicious stew, and hunks of freshly-made bread. After they had refreshed themselves, they learned that the place for which they were heading was not far away, and the woodcutter offered to show them the way. The offer was gratefully accepted and within the hour they were safe and sound at their hotel, and the woodcutter was back in his cottage with a suitable reward. When they were in the privacy of their room, the foaf could contain his curiosity no longer, and said to his friend: 'What was that you put in your pocket when we were eating the stew?' His friend pulled it out and they studied it in fascinated amazement: there was no doubt about it – it was a human fingernail.

A foaf went into an Indian restaurant and ordered a chicken curry. When it came, he saw instantly that, though there were pieces of chicken-skin in the gravy, the meat was in fact cat. How did he know? Well, he happens to be a professor of veterinary anatomy in the university.

Every university town has its Indian restaurant serving cats. ('We serve anybody, sir. Sit down.') If there isn't a chair of veterinary anatomy, well, there are always visiting professors. The foregoing has cropped up perpetually during my 20+ years of curryeating; last year I heard an interesting variation.

Three of us went on a milk round to one of the larger Northern Universities; Robert, whose alma matter it was assured Janet and I that, if we hadn't eaten at a certain Indian restaurant, we hadn't lived. It was with unrestrained eagerness that we allowed him to pilot us to the unforgettable eating-house, and we certainly haven't forgotten it. It stood in the middle of a site cleared for development, and we picked our way towards it: its lights shone out like a guiding beacon over the rubble. A 'waiter' with an unbelievable overall pointed to the only table of the two which was vacant. It was fastened to the ground, as were the stools – presumably the delicate balance of the layout would have been upset if clients had dared to move the furniture. The menu was written up on a blackboard, and there were in effect nine dishes: chicken, meat or egg; hot, medium or mild. I ordered hot egg, and waited to see what would happen. It came in a battered aluminium bowl, along with a plate of rice. In the bowl was some very hot curry gravy; a fried egg floating on the top, and some cabbage leaves underneath. It was very tasty, and the three of us feasted for a sum too little to have fed one at any normal restaurant. When we had finished, our proud demonstrator said: 'There's a very interesting story I heard about that place.' We couldn't wait. 'During my last year here, their deep-freeze was found to be full of alsatian carcasses. The public health people tried to prosecute, but the restaurant was offering "meat", and alsatian is "meat", so they got away with it.'

Such is the process of law. Subsequently, I heard the tale in two other northern towns.

Without letting on that we'd been there, Janet and I asked one our interviewees the following day if he knew of the place. 'God, yes,' he replied. 'There's a story about a student here who ate there every day, and at the end of his three years he had to go into hospital to have his guts rebuilt.'

Not that Indian restaurants are the only ones where odd things happen. A foaf was the wife of a sometime British Consul in Hong Kong. Apparently, she had gone into a Chinese restaurant with her little poodle, been ushered to a table, and indicated that she would like her dog to be fed as well. The inscrutable waiter took the dog to the inner regions, and in due time it was returned to its mistress, as a succulent dish, dressed like a sucking-pig with its bejewelled collar in its mouth.

Chows, I'm told, were bred for eating, which may be the origin of this story. And of course it is well-known that on Polar expeditions the Huskies are made use of as meat, so this WTS has a genuine pedigree.

Cats in Indian restaurants? Is it true that Indians eat Kite-Kat? Why not, it's quite wholesome. Where does fact end and fiction begin? There was the famous restaurant which served rat as a delicacy (61). There is more than one case of a prosecution for having live chickens in the kitchen.

A few notes on chickens. A foaf was feeding some chickens on behalf of a friend of his, who was away on holiday. The foaf was particularly upset by one of them, which would keep pecking his legs. Eventually, he took up the nearest thing to hand (which happened to be a billhook) and threw it at the importunate bird. Although the bird was decapitated, it ran around for *fully five minutes*.

Five minutes? Not very long. On 14th November, 1904, one Herbert V. Hughes, the proprietor of the Belvedere Hotel of Sault Ste Marie, Michigan, was killing chickens for Sunday dinner in the usual way. His kitchen maid was picking and cleaning them, when suddenly she fled screaming in terror. A black Minorca chicken was walking slowly round the room. The problem was that it was headless. The hen refused to die, and naturally attracted much publicity, drawing crowds to the Belvedere Hotel. Mr Hughes fed the chicken by means of a syringe 'injected into the raw end of the food pipe'. The hen would walk about, flap her wings, and go through the motions of stretching up and smoothing her feathers just as though her head were still there. 'At other times she would turn on her perch, sit down and get up and turn again, and at other times tried to croak or sing. She appeared not to suffer pain and to be as happy and contented as any hen.

'The chicken lived until 30th November, seventeen days after her head was cut off, and might have lived longer but for the fact that a "careless attendant" allowed the end of her neck to heal over the end of the windpipe and choke her to death.'

Careless indeed, since the hen was clearly a first-class draw (!) for the Belvedere Hotel. The story of the Belvedere chicken (74) is accompanied by two more.

Mr Wm. Hinkleman, who lives in California, states:

'many years ago on a ranch near Modesto I cut the head completely off a chicken and the chicken lived over a year. It was fed by a tube inserted in its neck and was on exhibition for some time in San Francisco.'

That one probably died of boredom. Another account was afforded by Mrs Mary Jane Beerup:

My father was killing and dressing a chicken for a country fair when he discovered one that he thought he had killed walking around with its head off. I fed it through its neck for several days and it is no telling how long it would have lived had it not caught its neck on a splinter and bled to death . . .

Tut, tut. Another careless attendant. Recently the production of chickens has increased enormously, and yet the number of headless ones strutting around appears to have dropped. But there will doubtless continue to be reports of them.

A classic WTS tells of an extraordinary incident on the East Lancs Road (A580). Apparently, a motorcyclist was riding behind a lorry which was carrying a load of thin steel plates. He decided to overtake the lorry, but as he moved out towards the centre of the road, one of the steel sheets became dislodged and decapitated him. However, his momentum carried him alongside the lorry, the lorry-driver glanced from his window, saw the headless motorcyclist passing, had a heart-attack, ran off the road and was killed.

The headless motorcyclist is, perhaps, a modern version of the headless horseman. Perhaps the original headless horseman (75) was Shah Ghazi Kaml of Bahu, Punjab, India. He lost his head in the battle of Jhajjar in 1635, but he did not sink lifeless from the saddle – his body was so securely seated that his trusty steed carried him home – a distance of some 26 miles. His body was lifted reverently from the saddle and placed in an ornate tomb – later a mosque and an artificial lake were added, and pilgrims have been visiting the place ever since.

It was back in the 1950s that a foaf was chased by a gang of teddy-boys while he was walking late one night along the promenade at Folkestone. Luckily, his car was not far away and he was an athletics Blue, so he sprinted for the vehicle, got in, started the engine and drove away just as his pursuers arrived. He heard an almightly BANG on the body, and there was a bit of a jerk, but he got safely away. When he arrived home, he got out to inspect the damage, and there, entangled in the rear-door handle was a bicycle chain, with a finger trapped in it. He went to the police, and via the hospital service they were able to trace the gang and take them to court.

This foaf was not the only one who has suffered such an attack. Another, in somewhat similar circumstances, managed to get away in his Volkswagen in the nick of time, but on this occasion the finger was trapped in the engine-grille at the rear. Another foaf was set upon in the Cambridge multi-storey car park, again managed to get away, and found a thumb stuck in the car door on arriving home.

However, all these incidents are trivial compared with another foaf who managed to reach his car, but couldn't get away in time. The thugs rocked the car, and banged on the roof, and lifted it up by the rear bumper. But they made a mistake: it was a front-wheel drive, and the foaf was able to get away with some struggle. When he inspected the damage, he found a hand caught under the bumper. Of course, he went to the police, and they made extensive inquiries, but after some weeks there was no news. They advised him to forget all about it.

It happens in America as well, and it may be that the subject of the next story is the same as he in the last. The foaf at last managed to fix a date with a girl he'd admired from afar for some time; they visit a movie, and then go for a car-ride, pull off the road, turn off the lights and find some sweet music on the radio. However, just as things are starting to happen, the sweet music is interrupted for a news-flash about an escaped sex-maniac with a hook arm. Now this upsets the girl greatly because she has visions of the man coming to get them, and nothing the foaf can say will persuade her otherwise, so he agrees to take her home. The car seems to be stuck in the mud, but he revs up and manages to get on to the highway and takes her home. He goes round to open the door for her and there, hanging on the handle, is a hook . . .

A friend of mine was told of the same species of experience by two other people; one said that it had happened in this country and the other that it happened in Italy. It seems that in each case, the girl was motoring with her boy-friend, when the car ran out of petrol. It was late at night, but they had passed an all-night garage not far back, and he had a can with him, so he decided to walk back. The girl locked the doors and curled up on the back seat. She was rudely awoken by someone rocking the car and banging on the roof. This went on and on – she huddled under a blanket too frightened to do anything. The interference stopped as abruptly as it started, and she dropped into an uneasy and uncomfortable sleep. Then she was awoken by more knockings and shouts of 'Open up, police.' Having warily ascertained that it was indeed the police, she opened the door, and allowed herself to be carried away. Later she found that her boy-friend had never left the vicinity; outside the car he had been set upon by a madman who had decapitated him, using the vehicle as an operating table.

There are worse versions. In another, the boy-friend is decapitated and hung from a tree over the car, and it is his shoes which go 'bang, bang, bang' on the car roof all night. And sometimes the decapitated body is hung upside-down . . .

Sometimes, the decapitation takes place in a university hall of residence: frightened girls are huddled in a room while horrific noises are heard outside. In the morning, the decapitated body is found in the passage.

Or again, a girl gets home late from a dance, and doesn't discover until morning that her room-mate – who didn't go to the dance, and whom she thought was asleep when she arrived home – has in fact been mutilated in her bed. Or worse still, the blood-thirsty maniac was actually hiding in the room when the latecomer returned. And sometimes, she turns on the light and discovers him behind the door with a bloody axe. The rationale of these stories is surely wonderful to consider.

A most unfortunate incident occurred last year (and the year before, and the year before that) in fact there ought to be pressure for a ban on Guy Fawkes, as on fireworks. It seems that to meet the increasing competition for bigger and better guys, a group of boys dressed one of their number in suitable clothes and installed him in the cart. As they processed along the High Street, they came to a butcher's shop, and crowded in with the inflationary demand '5p for the guy'. The butcher, however, had been plagued with such demands, and taking up a sharp knife laid into the 'effigy', stabbing it repeatedly. The charge, of course, was manslaughter.

At the beginning of the war, a young mother sailed for Ireland with her two young children, a girl of five and a baby of two. She was trying to settle them in their bunks for the night so that she could go off for dinner, but the baby refused to stop crying. In desperation, she shouted: 'If you don't shut up, I'll put you out of the porthole.' This seemed to quiet the child, and she went for her meal. When she returned, the porthole was open, the baby was gone, and her daughter slept blissfully.

For our closing story, there is another harassed mum with two children – the small boy and the larger girl. This time, she shouts: 'If you don't go to sleep I'll ... I'll ... cut off your willie.' This threat seems to work, so she goes downstairs and relaxes with a suitable glass. Then there is a scream from withup, and she rushes to the foot of the stairs to be greeted with her angelic daughter, brandishing a pair of dressmaking scissors, saying: 'He didn't keep quiet, so I cut it off for you.' To the hospital quickly! Mum grabs him from the cot, wraps him in a blanket and rushes down stairs, shouting to her daughter: 'You'd better come with me so that I can keep an eye on you.' She runs out to the garage, open the doors and lays her son on the back seat. Then she climbs in, reverses out of the garage, and runs over her daughter.

Bibliography

1 ACKERMANN, A. *Popular fallacies explained and corrected.* London, 1924.
2 ASH, Russell. *Fact or fiction?* A dossier on old beliefs that die hard. London, 1973.
3 ASIMOV, Isaac. 'Jokester' in *Earth is room enough.* London, 1960.
4 BEARD, Mrs L. Letter: *Observer.* 13th February, 1977.
5 BELLOC-LOWNDES, Mrs [Marie Adelaide]. *The end of her honeymoon.* London, 1913.
6 BETT, Henry. *English myths and traditions.* London, 1952.
7 The HOLY BIBLE: Apocrypha. *Bel and the dragon.*
8 BONAPARTE, Marie [Princess George of Greece]. *Myths of war* (Trans. J. Rodker). London, 1947.
9 BREWER, The Rev. Dr. *Dr Brewer's guide to science* A guide to the scientific knowledge of things familiar. London, 1865.
10 BRIGGS, Katharine M. *A dictionary of British folk-tales in the English language* Including the F. J. Norton collection. 4 Vols. London, 1970–1.
11 BRIGGS, Katharine M. and Tongue, R. L. (Eds.). *Folktales of England.* With a foreword by R. M. Dorson. London, 1969.
12 BULLEN, Frank T. *Creatures of the sea.* Being the life stories of some sea birds, beasts and fishes. London, 1904.
13 BULLEN, Frank T. *The cruise of the 'Cachalot'.* Round the world after sperm whales. London, 1898.
14 BURLAND, Cottie Arthur. *Myths of life and death.* London, 1974.
15 BURTON, Maurice and BURTON, Robert. *Inside the animal world.* London, 1977.
16 CAMPBELL, Joseph. *Myths to live by.* London, 1973.
17 *Cassell's book of humorous quotations.* Selected and arranged by A. K. Adams. London, 1969.
18 CHARLES, Robert H. (Trans.). *The Book of Jubilees.* London, 1917.
19 CHESTERTON, Gilbert K. 'The Blue Cross' in *The innocence of Father Brown.* London, 1916.
20 COLES, Manning (Pseud = Adelaide F. O. Manning+M. Coles). *Pray Silence.* London, 1940.
21 CONSTABLE, Ronnie in *Equipment design for the catering industry.* Ed. George Glew. London, 1977.

22 DALE, Rodney, A. M. *Louis Wain: the man who drew cats*. London, 1968/78.

23 DALI, Salvador. *The secret life of Salvador Dali*. Trans. Haakon M. Chevalier. London, 1968.

24 DAWE, Clyde J. *Tumours in aquatic mammals*. London, 1976.

25 DICKENS, Charles. *Bleak House*. London, 1852.

26 *Dictionary of National Biography*. London, 1885.

27 EARL, L. *Speeding north with the 'Royal Scot'*. A day in the life of a locomotive man. London, 1939.

28 EMRICH, Duncan. *Folklore on the American land*. Boston [Mass], 1972.

29 ERNSTING, Walter. *The day the gods died*. Trans. Wendayne Ackerman, London, 1977.

30 EVANS, Bergen. *The natural history of nonsense*. London, 1947.

31 EVANS, Bergen. *The spoor of spooks*. London, 1955.

32 EYRE-TODD, George (Trans.) *The Bruce*. Being the metrical history of Robert the Bruce, King of Scots, compiled AD 1375 by John Barbour. London, 1907.

33 *Folklore*. Indiana University Publications. 1940.

34 FURNISS, Harry. *Confessions of a caricaturist*. 2 Vols. London, 1901.

35 GARFIELD, Sydney. *Teeth, teeth, teeth*. London, 1972.

36 GLAISTER, J. *Medical jurisprudence and toxicology*. Eds. Edgar Rentoul and Hamilton Smith, 13th edn. London, 1973.

37 GOULD, George M. and PYLE, Walter L. *Anomalies and curiosities of medicine*. Philadelphia, 1897.

38 GRAY, Joan K. 'Some Cambridgeshire ghosts'. *Interface*, Vol. 10 No. 2 pp. 14–17. Cambridge, 1976.

39 GRUNDY. *Punch*, June 8 (p. 106) and June 29 (p. 232). 1977.

40 *The Guinness book of records*. Ed. Norris McWhirter, 23rd edn. London, 1976.

41 HAMMERTON, Sir John A. *As the days go by*. Leaves from my war diary 1939–40. London, 1941.

42 HARRISON, Michael. *Fire from heaven*. London, 1976.

43 HAWKINS, Gerald S. *Stonehenge decoded*. London, 1970.

44 HEIM, Alice W. 'An experiment on humour'. *Brit. J. Psych*, Vol. 27, pp. 141–61. 1936.

45 HEIM, Alice W. *Intelligence and personality*. London, 1970.

46 HERSEY, John. *Hiroshima*. London, 1946.

47 HOFFNUNG, Gerard. *Hoffnung at the Oxford Union: The Bricklayer*. Decca record DFE 8682. 1958.

48 HOGG, Ian & WEEKS, John. *Military small-arms of the twentieth centuy*, 2nd edn. London, 1973.

49 JONES, R. V. *Most secret war*. London, 1977.

50 LEE, Ken. *Happy as a sandbag*: A musical.

51 LEGMAN, G. *The rationale of the dirty joke*. 2 Vols. London, 1972.

52 LE POER TRENCH, William Francis Brinsley. *Secret of the ages*. UFOs from inside the earth. London, 1974.

53 LIEPMAN, Heinz. *Rasputin – a new judgment*. Trans. Edward Fitzgerald. London, 1959.

54 MACKAY, Alan L. *The harvest of a quiet eye*. A selection of scientific quotations. London, 1977.

55 MARRYAT, Capt. Frederick. *Jacob Faithful*. London, 1834.

56 MAYHEW, Henry. *Mayhew's London*. Ed. Peter Quennell. London, 1959.

57 MELLY, George. *Owning up*. London, 1965.

58 MILES, John A. 'Laughing at the Bible: Jonah as a parody'. *Jewish Quarterly Review*. January, 1975.

59 MINNEY, Rubeigh James. *Rasputin*. London, 1972.

60 Lord MONTAGU of Beaulieu. *The gilt and the gingerbread*. London, 1967.

61 MORRIS, Simon. 'Hot rats'. *Oz*, No. 44. September, 1972.

62 MUGGERIDGE, Malcolm and KINGSMILL, Hugh. *Brave old world*. London, 1936.

63 MUNCHAUSEN, Baron [Pseud]. *The travels and surprising adventures of Baron Munchausen*.

64 PARASCIENCE: feature in *New Scientist*, Vol. 75, No. 1060, pp. 74–83. 14th July, 1977.

65 PARSONS, Denys. *All too true*. London, 1954.

66 PARTRIDGE, Eric. *The 'shaggy dog' story*. Its origin, development and nature. London, 1954.

67 POE, Edgar Allan. *The popular tales of Edgar Allan Poe*. London, n.d.

68 POPE-HENNESSY, James. *Queen Mary 1867–1953*. London, 1959.

69 PORTER, Enid M. *Cambridgeshire customs and folklore*. London, 1969.

70 POTTER, Stephen. *Lifemanship, One-upmanship*. London, 1950, 1952.

71 PROTHEROE, Ernest. *The handy natural history of mammals*. London, 1909.

72 RATTIGAN, Terence. *Flare Path*.

73 REYNOLDS, Stanley. 'When the Southland gave birth to the blues'. *Radio Times*. 13th–19th November, 1976.

74 RIPLEY, Robert L. *The omnibus believe it or not*. London, 1935.

75 RIPLEY, Robert L. *The mammoth believe it or not*. London, 1956.

76 RISING, Lawrence. *She who was Helen Cass*.

77 SANDERS, Dierdre *et al*. *Would you believe it?* London, 1973.

78 SASSOON, George T. and DALE, Rodney, A. M. *The manna machine*. London, 1978.

79 SEABROOK, Jeremy. 'A change in atmosphere: race in one town'. *New Society*, Vol. 37, pp. 486–91. 2nd September, 1976.

80 SHARP, Gerald. *The seige of Ladysmith*. London, 1976.

81 SHAW, George Bernard. *Androcles and the lion.*

82 SMITH, H. Allen. *The compleat practical joker.* London, 1954.

83 SPERLING, Harry and SIMON, Maurice (Trans.). *The Zohar,* 5 Vols. London, 1931–4.

84 SQUIERS, Granville. *Secret hiding places.* London, 1933.

85 SUTHERLAND, James (Ed.). *The Oxford book of literary anecdotes.* Oxford, 1975.

86 SYMONS, Julian G. *Buller's campaign.* London, 1963.

87 THOMPSON, Stith. *Motif-index of folk-literature.* 6 Vols. Copenhagen, 1955.

88 TRACHTENBERG, Joshua. *The devil and the Jews.* New Haven, 1945.

89 TURNER, Ernest S. *The phoney war on the home front.* London, 1961.

90 WALTERS, Cumine (Ed.). *Bygone Suffolk.* London, 1901.

91 WATSON, Lyall. *The Romeo error.* London, 1974.

92 WAY, R. *Antique dealer.* London, 1957.

93 WIGRAM, George V. *Englishman's Hebrew and Chaldee concordance to the Old Testament.* London, 1860 (repr.).

94 WILSON, Colin. *Rasputin and the fall of the Romanovs.* London, 1964.

95 WOOD, Rev. J. G. *The popular natural history.*

96 WOOLLCOTT, Alexander. *While Rome burns.* London, 1934.

ADDENDA

97 WARD, Philip. *A dictionary of common fallacies.* Cambridge 1978.

98 WATSON, Rev. John Selby. *Reasoning power in animals.* London 1867.

Index

I cannot believe that I am the only person in the world who finds it necessary to be perpetually leaping up from the meal-table to exact some apposite reference from his library. Fellow-leapers will know only too well that half an index is often worse than no index at all, and that inadequacy in this department results in one's return, empty-handed, to an anapolaustic table of wrath.

What follows is my attempt to obviate your having to eat a congealing meal while the others are washing-up. Perhaps it's not such a good idea after all . . .

161

personified, 48
Mince quietens gearbox, 125
Ministry of Information; fatuous bomb rumour retracted, 115; rumours of firing sea, 115
Miracle of Fatima, 121
Mishearings, 36
Mistaken identity; ashes for spice, 41; books for whisky, 40; camel dung for hash, 41; caravanner, 38; day tripper, 128; driving tester, 125; kindly mechanic, 129; owner of Triumph, 40; plumber, 37; specimens, 41
Mole, hydatidiform, 76
Monkey Business, 34
Montagu, Lord; quoted, 127
Moon-landing, gigantic hoax, 121
More, Kenneth; lands on moon, 121
Morgan, A Suitable Case for Treatment, 35
Mortuary attendants, 68; eating off floor, 69
Mother, harassed; children mutilated, 151
Motor-car borrowed as burglary decoy, 129; commits suttee, 125; damaged by elephant, 135; damages attacker, 149; collects human parts, 149; gearbox silenced, 215; passion-waggon dismantled, 125; purchased for £5, 123; relieving oneself against, 29; ritual dismantling, 127; role in society, 123; traps elephant's trunk, 137

Motorcyclist; headless, 148; injures driving tester, 125
Mouse crushed by bride, 138; sausages, 143
Multiple birth; The Hague, 1276, 76
Munchausen, Baron; cloak becomes rabid, 140; wolf pulls sledge, 140; postilion's music freezes, 140
Murals crumbling, 51
Music frozen, released by warmth, 140
Mystery tour mistake, 128

Napoleon Bonaparte; insomniac, 83
Nelson, Lord; pickled in brandy, 65
Neologisms defined; foaf, 13; head-dropper, 32, 77; Valdemar, to, 51; wenge, 25
Newfie jokes, 19
New York; alligators in sewers, 58; power failure, 110
North sea oil a myth, 114
Nostradamus improved by admirers, 94, 103
Nun; Flambeau disguised as, 100
Nuns as spies, 100
Nurse nurtures snake in stomach, 74

Obeyesekera, Rita Bandaranaike; parcels person, 87
Objets trouvés crumbling, 51
Octopus causes pregnancy, 74
Old wives' tales defined and exemplified, 26

163

Tailpiece

As I hinted in the Prologue, I am willing to receive and classify both new WTSs and variants on old ones; indeed, many have come my way since I completed this text.

The 'couple stuck in the car' (page 126) for example, which was in Southport at the end of 1976, had reached Cambridge by May 1977, and London by the end of the year; according to the BBC, it happened in Regent's Park, complete with the WRVS handing out tea to the assembled crowds.

That sounds like a travelling WTS; on the other hand, I have personal knowledge of the case of a 'police car running into the back of the testee' (page 124), although I first heard the *story* in the early 1950s.

So there are just two examples of the changing panorama of the WTS; I have no doubt that there are scores of others. Contributions should be sent to: Editorial Department, Wyndham Publications, 44 Hill Street, London W1X 8LB.

HUMOUR

0352	Star	
300698	Woody Allen **GETTING EVEN**	50p*
398973	Alida Baxter **FLAT ON MY BACK**	50p
397187	**OUT ON MY EAR**	60p
397101	**UP TO MY NECK**	50p
301139	**TWO'S COMPANY**	60p ◆
301511	Nicolas Bentley **PAY BED**	60p
301104	Peter Buchanan **THE RAG TRADE**	60p ◆
301708	Max Bygraves **THE MILKMAN'S ON HIS WAY**	70p
301090	John Cleese, Jack Hobbs & Joe McGrath **THE STRANGE CASE OF THE END OF CIVILISATION AS WE KNOW IT**	95p ◆
396245	David Dawson **VET IN DOWNLAND**	60p
302097	**VET IN THE VALE**	60p
395494	Les Dawson **A CARD FOR THE CLUBS**	60p
397632	**THE SPY WHO CAME**	50p*
398612	Alex Duncan **IT'S A VET'S LIFE**	60p
398795	**THE VET HAS NINE LIVES**	50p
395389	**VETS IN CONGRESS**	60p
395699	**VET AMONG THE PIGEONS**	60p
397020	**VETS IN THE BELFRY**	50p
396016	Andre Launay **COME INTO MY BED**	60p
397780	Spike Milligan **THE GREAT McGONAGALL SCRAPBOOK**	75p
396407	**MILLIGAN'S BOOK OF RECORDS**	75p
395907	Stanley Morgan **A BLOW FOR GABRIEL HORN**	70p
396237	**INSIDE ALBERT SHIFTY**	70p
398965	**RUSS TOBIN'S BEDSIDE GUIDE TO SMOOTHER SEDUCTION**	60p
397454	**THE FLY BOYS: SKY-JACKED**	70p
395370	**RANDY COMFORT RISE AGAIN**	70p
395591	**RUSS TOBIN: HARD UP**	70p
30118X	**RUSS TOBIN: UP TIGHT**	70p

† For sale in Britain and Ireland only.
*Not for sale in Canada.
◆ Film & T.V. tie-ins.

GENERAL FICTION

0352	Star	
301481	Michael J. Bird **WHO PAYS THE FERRYMAN?**	85p ♦
39613X	William Burroughs **DEAD FINGERS TALK**	75p
395621	Jackie Collins **THE STUD**	65p
300701	**LOVEHEAD**	70p
398663	**THE WORLD IS FULL OF DIVORCED WOMEN**	50p
398752	**THE WORLD IS FULL OF MARRIED MEN**	50p
396113	Robertson Davies **FIFTH BUSINESS**	95p
396881	Alexander Edwards **A STAR IS BORN**	60p ♦
30166X	Robert Grossbach **THE GOODBYE GIRL**	60p* ♦
301406	W. Harris **SALIVA**	70p
302100	Dan Jenkins **SEMI-TOUGH**	75p* ♦
398981	Jeffrey Konvitz **THE SENTINEL**	70p* ♦
301643	Dean R. Koontz **NIGHT CHILLS**	75p*
396903	Lee Mackenzie **EMMERDALE FARM (No. 1) THE LEGACY**	50p ♦
396296	**EMMERDALE FARM (No. 2) PRODIGAL'S PROGRESS**	60p ♦
395974	**EMMERDALE FARM (No. 3) ALL THAT A MAN HAS . . .**	60p ♦
301414	**EMMERDALE FARM (No. 4) LOVERS' MEETING**	60p ♦
301422	**EMMERDALE FARM (No. 5) A SAD AND HAPPY SUMMER**	60p ♦
396164	Graham Masterton **THE MANITOU**	70p ♦
39526 5	**THE DJINN**	75p*

† For sale in Britain and Ireland only.
*Not for sale in Canada.
♦ Film & T.V. tie-ins.

GENERAL FICTION

0352	397403	Robert Stone **DOG SOLDIERS**	75p*
	395427	Peter Upton **GREEN HILL FAR AWAY**	95p
	301570	Margaret Walker **JUBILEE**	95p*
	301562	N. Richard Nash **EAST WIND, RAIN**	95p*
	395540	Gail Parent **DAVID MEYER IS A MOTHER**	70p
	300809	Molly Parkin **LOVE ALL**	50p
	397179	**UP TIGHT**	60p
	396288	Erich Maria Remarque **BOBBY DEERFIELD**	85p* ♦
	396946	Judith Rossner **TO THE PRECIPICE**	85p*
	302089	**NINE MONTHS IN THE LIFE OF AN OLD MAID**	75p*
	398892	Alan Sillitoe **THE GENERAL**	50p
	300965	**THE LONELINESS OF THE LONG–DISTANCE RUNNER**	50p
	300949	**MEN, WOMEN AND CHILDREN**	50p
	300981	**SATURDAY NIGHT AND SUNDAY MORNING**	50p
	395141	**THE WIDOWER'S SON**	85p
	397144	**THE FLAME OF LIFE**	70p
	398809	**THE RAGMAN'S DAUGHTER**	50p
	396415	Hubert Selby Jr. **THE ROOM**	75p

GENERAL NON-FICTION

0352   Star

301392	Linda Blandford **OIL SHEIKHS**	95p
396121	Anthony Cave Brown **BODYGUARD OF LIES (Large Format)**	£1.95*
301368	John Dean **BLIND AMBITION**	£1.00*
300124	Dr. F. Dodson **HOW TO PARENT**	75p*.
301457	**THE FAMILY DICTIONARY OF SYMPTOMS**	95p†
398914	J. Paul Getty **HOW TO BE RICH**	60p*
397829	**HOW TO BE A SUCCESSFUL EXECUTIVE**	60p*
398566	Harry Lorayne & Jerry Lucas **THE MEMORY BOOK**	60p*
39692X	Henry Miller **THE WORLD OF SEX**	60p
395311	Neville Randall & Gary Keane **FOCUS ON FACT:** **THE WORLD OF INVENTION (illus)**	75p
39532X	**THE STORY OF SPORT (illus)**	75p
39529X	**THE PSYCHIC WORLD (illus)**	75p
395303	**THE STORY OF CHRISTMAS (illus)**	75p
395338	**UNSOLVED MYSTERIES (illus)**	75p
397640	David Reuben **HOW TO GET MORE OUT OF SEX**	85p*
398779	Fiona Richmond **FIONA**	50p
396040	Idries Shah **THE SUFIS (Large Format)**	£1.95
395478	Michael Smith **THE DUCHESS OF DUKE STREET** **ENTERTAINS**	£1.50♦

Wyndham Books are obtainable from many booksellers and newsagents. If you have any difficulty please send purchase price plus postage on the scale below to:

Wyndham Cash Sales,
PO Box 11,
Falmouth,
Cornwall.

While every effort is made to keep prices low, it is sometimes necessary to increase prices at short notice. Wyndham Books reserve the right to show new retail prices on covers which may differ from those advertised in the text or elsewhere.

Postage and Packing Rate
U.K.
One book 22p plus 10p per copy for each additional book ordered to a maximum charge of 82p.

B.F.P.O. & Eire
One book 22p plus 10p per copy for the next 6 books, and thereafter 4p per book.

Overseas
One book 30p plus 10p per copy for each additional book.

These charges are subject to Post Office charge fluctuations